# You, the Teacher

# You, the Teacher

By
Lawrence O. Richards

MOODY PRESS
CHICAGO

© 1972 by
THE MOODY BIBLE INSTITUTE
OF CHICAGO

All scripture quotations, unless otherwise noted, are from J. B. Phillips's **New Testament in Modern English** and are used by permission of the Macmillan Company, New York City.

The use of selected references from various versions of the Bible in this publication does not necessarily imply publisher endorsement of the versions in their entirety.

Library of Congress Catalog Card Number: 72-77942

ISBN: 0-8024-9829-9

**Printed in the United States of America**

*To Naomi
and all the teachers whom
God will bless through
this, her story.*

## Contents

| Chapter | Page |
|---|---|
| Introduction: About You, the Teacher | 9 |
| 1. I Know a Teacher | 11 |
| 2. You're Unique | 25 |
| 3. Life on the Upswing | 37 |
| 4. Called to Care | 47 |
| 5. Called to Teach | 59 |
| 6. Responding | 73 |
| 7. Around the Table | 87 |
| 8. Stepping Beyond | 101 |
| 9. In Our Sunday School? | 113 |
| 10. You, the Teacher | 121 |

# About You, the Teacher

There are many books about teaching but not so many about you, the teacher.

This book is about you.

It won't go into detail about what you *do* in teaching. (I've another Moody Press book, *Creative Bible Teaching,* that does just that.) But it will go into detail about what you *are* as a teacher of God's Word, about how God works through you in communicating the love of Jesus, and about the relationship you develop with your students that reveals most clearly the reality of the faith you teach—and represent.

This book is about you, a teacher, a person through whom the Teacher, our Lord, reaches out to touch and to transform others who are so deeply loved by Him.

# 1

I Know a Teacher

I suppose we can all agree that being a Sunday school teacher is something special.
We should.
And then, every once in a while, we get to know a **really** special teacher, a teacher God uses in a special way to make Christ so real to his or her students that they respond to Him, they grow as Christians, and their lives are transformed.
I know such a teacher.
Her name is Naomi.
This is her story, exactly as she told it.

## I Know a Teacher

I was reared in a preacher's home; and in my experience with Sunday school, I always felt that teachers were teaching more for a reward from the pastor and other people in the church. I was put into a teaching position when I was very young, and forced to become a leader in the church. But after nineteen years in a Christian home and a year and a half of Christian college, by the time I married and had two children of my own, I just was beginning to question the whole thing—God in general and all the specifics that go with it. I was feeling that everything I'd ever experienced was really phoney. I found that the people that had been teaching me—relating to me as far as Christianity goes—really had nothing to offer and that I really had nothing to offer anybody else. About that time our Sunday school superintendent asked me if I would teach the second grade class.

I didn't quite have the courage to refuse, because I knew if I did I'd have to explain why I was refusing; and really, well, I was partly afraid of my husband's reaction. I took the class and began teaching the way that I was accustomed to and the way that other teachers had taught me. I sat in on some other classes, and it was the same old thing; so I thought I would go along with it, and maybe I'd feel better about it later.

About the third Sunday that I was teaching, the story was the one in the Old Testament about moving the ark of the covenant, and the man who reached his hand out and was killed. The story had always upset me, even when I was a child. So I called Pastor Howard's wife and told her that I was very disturbed. I said I'd rather give the class up, because this is supposed to be part of the Bible and I hated the story. Her reaction was exactly what I didn't want, because she said, "OK, if you really don't want to teach that story don't. Teach something else."

I wanted her to say, "It's part of the Bible. You better accept it and teach it, or else quit." She didn't say that, and I came home quite disturbed. At that point I felt, if God was really there and really had supervised the writing of the Bible, there had to be a reason for that story. So I asked Him as simply as I could to help me forget the whole past and show me just why this happened.

I started to read the story and to read the events before and after, and got very involved with the study. Through the Holy Spirit, the Lord showed me so clearly that this was the essence of God Himself, that he was trying to show His people His holiness and glory, and that relationship with Him had to be on a special level—that He was a *holy* God. And it had never been related to me like that. It had been, "You touched the ark! So God is punishing you for disobeying." That affected my whole life. It was the beginning of realizing that much of what I had experienced really was phoney. So when I taught, I admitted to my girls that this story had been hard for me to understand. I had never admitted anything like that when I was teaching, but I just told them this had been a very difficult story for me to accept.

Afterward I asked them about the ark. They all seemed to really understand. It was so exciting to me that I had been able to communicate what I had learned and experienced. So at that point I told the Lord that I felt ineffective as a teacher and that I hadn't really experienced any teachers that I thought had really communicated His love and grace to me, but that I wanted Him, through the Holy Spirit, to teach those kids and let me be involved in the learning.

At that point, I guess, so many things started to happen. But the basic thing was that my whole motivation changed. I was no longer really concerned that Pastor Howard knew I was there every Sunday. I no longer cared about the pat on the back for teaching and all that, which had been extremely important to me before. My motivation was for learning. Experiencing became really Christ-centered, and I just had a totally different attitude toward those kids. I was so involved with them and concerned for them, and I *loved* them just like my own kids, really. There were several kids in the class who were totally indifferent to everything. "Oh, we've heard that story seventeen times"; you know, that sort of thing. So I stopped telling a Bible story just to tell a Bible story. I would read the story at home and really study it thoroughly and watch God and see if I could understand why He put the story in the Bible to start with, what was practical about this for our lives, and why He did what He did in the story. And I tried to communicate this to the kids, instead of just telling stories.

Sometimes I'd start talking to them, and I could see that there were too many things bugging them from last week; so I'd forget the story, and we'd sit in a circle and talk about these things openly.

I never told the kids things that were too personal to share with them; but on a Sunday morning when Paul and I had just had a knock-down, drag-out fight on the way to church, I couldn't see coming in and behaving like everything was right between God and me when it wasn't. One time, in fact, I got there and started in on the lesson. It was a story on Christ's life, when He was expressing to His disciples that one of the most important things He desired from them was not sacrifice but a whole new mental attitude. And all of a sudden I realized that what I was doing was what Christ was telling His disciples He really hated! So I stopped right in the middle and told the kids that I felt I had really been unreasonable with Paul, and I asked them to pray for me. And they did. You know, we were just sitting around in a circle, and we did things like that. I don't know if they ever discussed things like that with their parents; but I don't think they did, because I never got any feedback from the kids or their parents.

So I wasn't really in a teaching position. I filled them in on facts, when that was necessary and did as little of the lecture kind of thing as I could, and always gave them a chance to talk.

## Problems—and outreach

>Naomi's love for the kids and desire for deeper involvement did create problems with time and with curriculum. She hated to rush through story after story, and found that when she tried to give the girls a chance to talk, time seemed too short.

Really, I started teaching them doctrine. I told the pastor that I felt my girls needed to know as much about God as they could, because how could they trust Him if they didn't know what He was like? So I started with sovereignty, and we spent weeks and weeks on just one story—the story of Daniel when he was telling Nebuchadnezzar about the dream and how God showed Nebuchadnezzar that He *really* was sovereign; but He was so patient with him—a whole year after that dream before—well, you know.

The kids responded way beyond my expectations. I felt there was something there, but I was very shortsighted. And *they* taught me so much! In the story they would teach me things that I wouldn't see; and in areas of personal living and daily activities and everything, they could relate God's sovereignty to things that were hard for me to have much faith about. We started with sovereignty, and we went through justice, love, grace.

I was very concerned about the fact that after opening exercises, by the time we got to class, got roll taken, Bibles counted, and so on. I'd have half an hour. The other teachers were saying, "Can't we take the kids out to play? What are we going to do for half an hour? The story is only ten minutes." And I was just terribly frustrated because I didn't have *enough* time. I'd get in there, cram the story down their throats, pray for two minutes, and let them out the door. I felt really terrible because they had no chance to express themselves or get acquainted with one another.

The pastor's wife was in charge of the department at that time, so I asked if I could just *try* taking the kids for the whole time—from when they came to church until their parents left. She tried hard to understand me, and I know it was hard for her. So she told me she'd permit it only if I called each parent individually and got permission. Finally we decided to have the kids in the morning church service (which is before Sunday school at our church) until time for the sermon, and then come out. That still gave me an hour and a half.

We didn't have a whole "spiritual" hour and a half. We went outdoors and played together, and we did a lot of different things. Sometimes we made things, like on Father's Day. But the time the kids loved most was when we just sat in a circle to talk and really get acquainted and get into things pretty deeply.

One Christmas, I felt very strongly that the kids should have *something* that would help them experience what Christmas really means. So I went in search of a project. I called different places trying to find a needy family (which is the typical approach), and I didn't have much success. Sometimes it was a bad marriage or some other situation I couldn't take the kids into. So the parents started telling me, "Why don't you just collect money from the kids and *you* take it down there?" And I said, "That's exactly what I *don't* want to do."

So I finally got hold of the head of a mission, and he told me the name of a lady and her husband who had taken kids in, and at that time there were fifteen of them living in this little house. They're a very clean and wonderful family, and she's just one of those with a big heart that keeps taking people in. So I went down to visit her and to tell her the wonderful things we planned to do for her. She came to the door, and I told her who I was, and she was very cold to me. Then I went in and said pretty much what we wanted to do. And she said, "You know, I really think your motives are good. I don't question that. But if you are going to bring a bunch of spoiled rich kids down here to make these dear children feel less than they are, or less than the rich kids, keep your money and stay at home. We're perfectly content; we don't have a lot, but we're perfectly happy. We don't need your money."

It really clobbered me. I didn't know what to do. I could see what she was saying. So I came back to the kids; and I thought, *How will I ever tell the kids this?* I grappled with it all week, and I thought, *I've just got to think of some way to put it to them so they'll understand.* And the Lord just said out loud to me—practically, "Tell them what she said, stupid!" It was so crazy. So I did. And boy! They got it right away.

So I called the parents and told them, "Now don't you give your kids a *penny*. I want them to earn this money, and I want it to be all on their own."

Then we had a day when we got together—the kids and I— and baked everything. We weren't going to go out and buy food at all; we were going to make it all. And we made salads and homemade bread and cookies. The kids had a ball. We got all the money together that we had collected, and one Sunday we spent the whole time talking about what we thought we ought buy. We had the name and age and sex of each child. So they told me what they thought I should get, and I did the buying. Then we brought all the toys there and wrapped all the things that day, and the kids did everything. Then I told them that the following Wednesday we would all go down to the house.

Well, it was just fantastic. We had a whole camper full of kids and stuff—just jammed in there. We pulled up in front of the house, and I was a little nervous. But the kids weren't; they seemed very relaxed. They went in, and some of these little kids couldn't speak English; they spoke Spanish. And it wasn't ten minutes before the kids were coming to me and saying, "Couldn't they just unwrap *one* thing?"—after they met the kids.

We kept going back. Mrs. Carascious invited us back in January for a birthday party for one of the little girls. The kids would bring things; and when we got a couple boxes, we'd go back. They'd all play together and just have a ball. Even though they couldn't talk, they could laugh.

That was three years ago this Christmas that we first went, and we are still very close to this family. I go down there; in fact, I was just down there today. It's been very much a give-and-take situation. I respect her, I guess, more than anyone I know. I think she's just wonderful, and she knows I think that. So it's not a matter of my giving to her; we give to each other.

Anyway, one thing happened during that time that just really gave me a shot in the arm. They needed furniture desperately. The furniture was just a mess. And through the company where I'm a buyer, I have a good source for that. But I don't *own* the company; I can't just go in and take something. So I told the kids, "They very badly need a good hide-a-bed that they can use for the kids to sleep on. So let's start praying that the Lord will give a bed."

Well, I have to admit I was planning to finagle; and in my mind I was thinking, *I'll do this and this, and they'll think that God gave the hide-a-bed.* It was terrible, really; and I knew I was being dishonest. So one day, when I was on a buying trip, I stopped at a furniture manufacturer; and I thought, *Oh well, give it a try.* So I told the guy, "I want an Early American hide-a-bed. It has to be beige and green and rust and gold, it has to be queen size, and it has to be so much money."

So he looked up and down all the inventory sheets—and nothing. So he said, "The only thing I have that's close to that is a sofa and chair in those colors, but's it's not a hide-a-bed. And it's not a very good grade fabric, and it's so much money" —which was quite a bit more than I had.

I thought, *Well, that's better than nothing. Somehow I'll*

*get the rest of the money; I can't let the kids down. They're praying for this; I've got to answer their prayers.* So I told the guy, "I'll take it."

As soon as I said that—boy! It was just like the Lord jerked me by the arm. I knew immediately that I had done the wrong thing, but I was too proud to tell the salesman what was going on. So right about then he had to leave the room for something. As soon as he left and I was alone with God, I had to face it. I said, "OK, I see that's not the right thing to do, but what *am* I going to do? You'll have to show me."

The guy came back in a minute. He had gone in to the president of the company; and he just mentioned to him, "I have a buyer who wants a hide-a-bed," and gave the description. The president of the company said, "Would you believe we had one made up for my wife, and she doesn't like it? But it's not new, so I can't sell if for new. I'll give it to you for $90" (which happened to be less than the money I had to spend!). Then he said, "In fact, there's a chair in the inventory that was made up and then refused. It's green, and the back drops down and makes into a twin bed; and you can have that for so much." And this amounted to almost exactly what I had to spend!

I was so excited. I couldn't wait to get out. And I couldn't wait for Sunday morning. I was thrilled! I admitted to the kids that I hadn't really been very honest about it myself because I was trying to answer their prayer myself, and God just reached down and really answered it. And man, the kids— that's one thing they *did* go home and tell their parents.

Mrs. C. was so thrilled with it, she cried and everything! And I cried; and oh, it was really something. Because I told her what had happened; I said, "This isn't from me, and it's not from the kids. It's right from the Lord."

We also got her some carpeting and a dinette set about the same way. I hadn't ever really experienced answers to prayer like I did with that class.

And it hasn't stopped now that I'm teaching young teens. There's a girl in my class who had a friend whose parents were getting a divorce. She's superintelligent, and the girl in my class was very concerned for her. She said, "She's really an atheist"; and I said, "Why don't you bring her to Sunday school?"

She was very honest with me and said, "The way you talk, you're too relaxed, and things in the class would be hard for her."

And I said, "Well, my real reason for teaching Sunday school is to communicate to *you* how to communicate to *her*. I want you to experience how neat it is to really tell people about the Lord and just have it be your whole life, not a separate thing on Sunday."

So I called this girl in my class during the week, and I'd say, "I know you're praying for Sue. How are things going?" and so on. We did invite her to parties, and she did come to Sunday school a couple of times. I promised Pam, "If you bring her, I won't embarass her and I won't embarass you."

Graduation was in the spring. And the girl in my class, Pam, went into high school, and Sue was still just as far from the Lord as ever. Once in a while when I'd see Pam around church, I'd say, "How's Sue?" and she'd say, "Well, she's moving back East." Well, she finally got Sue to go to camp, and she met the Lord. After the sermon (it was the day Mr. Richards preached in church), I saw Pam and Sue and went back to say hello; and Pam said, "Oh, guess what. Sue met the Lord!" And I just went to pieces, and everybody was standing there looking at me as though I was crazy. Boy, that frustrates me, because I think it embarrasses the girls. I don't care myself, but I don't want them to be embarassed.

What was really neat about it was that Pam and I had really become close friends. And we had really prayed about Sue together and trusted the Lord for this. I realize that everyone we pray for isn't going to meet the Lord, but it was so neat how the Lord really did answer those prayers. And it drew Pam and me close together, even though she's not in my class anymore.

That's the thing. I just hate it when these kids leave and I never see them; I get so attached to them.

But now I have a whole new crop, and it's always the same thing. There are always those who know all the answers and are so bored. I just want to hug them and say, "Poor thing! Don't be bored; it's not boring." It's exciting to be starting all over again.

*You'll gain the most from reading this short book if you stop with me at the end of each chapter to react—and act.*

## REACT

1. Forget for a moment some of the things Naomi **did** as a teacher and think about her as a person. From what she has shared, what do you think she is like? Why not look over the chapter again and jot down some key words or phrases that picture **her.**
2. Think about yourself from the point of view of someone in her classes (the first class she decribes was a class of primaries—second graders). How do you think the children saw her? How did they feel about her?

## ACT

1. Take a moment to think about yourself—not what you **do** in your teaching but about the kind of person you are. What are you like? Jot down some key words or phrases that picture **you.**

2. Think about yourself from the point of view of your own Sunday school class. How do you think the children, youth, or adults you teach view you? How do they feel about you?

# 2
You're Unique

After nineteen years in a Christian home and a year and a half of Christian college, by the time I was married and had two children of my own, I just was beginning to question the whole thing—God in general and all the specifics that go with it. I was feeling that everything I'd ever experienced was really phoney. About that time our Sunday school superintendent asked me if I would teach the second grade class.

As Naomi began to teach, she was far from the "super Christian" some may feel the Sunday school teacher is supposed to be. Many experiences in her home and many contacts with others had influenced her, and she had become bitter and distrustful. "I found that the people that had been teaching me—relating to me as far as Christianity goes—really had nothing to offer, and that I really had nothing to offer anybody else."

Naomi knew herself to be far from God. Her bitterness, her anger, led her to "question the whole thing—God in general and all the specifics that go with it."

I'm sure that if her pastor had known where Naomi was as a person at that time, she'd not have been enlisted as a teacher. But perhaps Naomi started out her teaching career with an advantage; she started out realizing her need.

Have you ever wondered about the men Jesus chose to be His disciples, to follow Him in His own teaching and reaching ministry? They were a peculiar lot. Thomas could live with the Lord for three full years of His ministry, witness His miracles, and hear the intimate instruction He reserved for the twelve alone, and still—after hearing Christ foretell His resurrection and listening to the testimony of those who had seen the risen Lord—declare, "I will not believe, unless—" Thomas was a man to whom faith came hard. But Jesus chose him.

There were James and John. Once they put their mother up to asking the Lord to give them special places, over their ten companions, in His coming kingdom. They were the kind who are quick to think of their own advantage and to let the other man look out for himself. They showed this same trait when their little group journeyed across Samaria and was refused entry to a Samaritan town—quite a natural rejection from these traditional enemies. Flaming up in anger, James and John insisted Jesus call down fire from heaven to destroy the men who had insulted them—and to destroy the innocents in their families! Yes, James and John earned their nickname, "sons of thunder." James and John were men to whom love came hard. But Jesus chose them.

Then there was Levi, a Jew who could easily make a deal with Israel's conquerors to collect their taxes, and, as was the practice, in the collecting rake in as much or more for himself. Levi, later renamed Matthew, was classed by respectable society with prostitutes and other criminal elements.

Yes, Levi loved money more than God or man. But Jesus chose him.

And so it goes—even with Peter, the rough, blunt old fisherman. Once Jesus went aboard his boat to preach to a crowd that thronged the shores of Gennesaret. The Bible tells us,

> When he had finished speaking, he said to Simon, "Push out now into deep water and let down your nets for a catch."
> Simon replied, "Master! We've worked all night and never caught a thing, but if you say so I'll let the nets down."
> And when they had done this, they caught an enormous shoal of fish—so big that the nets began to tear. So they signaled to their friends in the other boat to come and help them. They came and filled both the boats to sinking point. When Simon Peter saw this, he fell on his knees before Jesus and said, "Keep away from me, Lord, for I'm only a sinful man!" (Lk 5:4-11).

Peter was a man to whom holiness came hard. But Jesus chose him.

Jesus chose persons who were imperfect, who were doubters, who were often angry and unloving, who were dishonest, who found close association with God painful. To teach others about Him, Jesus chose sinners.

## Why?

There are, of course, quick and easy answers as to why Jesus chose sinners to teach others about Him. For one thing, who else could He choose? The Bible's blunt "everyone falls short" makes it perfectly clear that every man Jesus met in

Palestine, every man or woman teaching in our Sunday schools today, has this in common. All of us are sinners. All of us have known warping of our personalities by that sin which infects our very nature. We're all doubters. We're all unloving. We're all greedy. We all, in ourselves, shrink back from God and His holiness. So Jesus had no other group to choose from.

Of course, He might have gone to a group of men who refused to *recognize* their sinfulness. He might have selected a Pharisee, who "trusted in himself that he was righteous." But this was the one kind of person Jesus' love could never touch.

Jesus had many confrontations with Pharisees. In all of them, these respectable members of society, the most "religious" of men, resisted and rejected God's beloved Son. One time after Jesus gave sight to a man blind from birth, the Pharisees, in a bitter fury, excommunicated him from the fellowship of Israel for his testimony of Jesus. Knowing the circumstances, Jesus remarked,

> "My coming into this world is itself a judgment—those who cannot see have their eyes opened and those who think they can see become blind."
>
> Some of the Pharisees near him overheard this and said, "So, we're blind, too, are we?"
>
> "If you were blind," returned Jesus, "nobody could blame you, but, as you insist 'We can see,' your guilt remains" (Jn 9:39-41).

At another time, the Pharisees and their companions kept muttering indignantly about the fact that Jesus was often surrounded by crowds of tax collectors. They challenged Jesus' disciples, saying,

> "Why do you have your meals with tax collectors and sinners?"
>
> [But here Jesus intervened.] "It is not the healthy who need the doctor, but those who are ill. I have not come to

invite the 'righteous' but the 'sinners'—to change their ways" (Lk 5:30-32).

Only the man who knows he is sick seeks out the healer. Only the man who is aware of his blindness cries out for light. Only the man who realizes his sin and his need turns to Jesus.

So there are always some people Christ's love cannot touch. For Christ's love is known first *only* as forgiveness. A Thomas, a James and John, a Peter—or a Naomi—who faces the darkness in his own personality can meet Jesus and respond to His love. But a Pharisee, a pretender who builds all sorts of barriers to hide from others and from himself, always turns away. To know Jesus' love, to accept it *as forgiveness,* would be to admit sin. And this the Pharisee can never do.

So we can understand why Jesus chose the men He did to be with Him and to become teachers. And we can understand something of what it takes for us to accept the title "teacher" today. It takes honesty with ourselves. It takes facing just how short we fall of all we should be. It takes a realization that the teacher is—and remains—a sinner.

## Forgiveness

It's exciting for me as a teacher—a human being who often falls short—to realize what forgiveness means and how it changes the way I live with and teach my classes.

The Bible gives us insight through this report of Jesus' conversation with a Pharisee who had invited Him to dinner. During the meal a woman known to be a prostitute came into the hall and, weeping, washed the road dust from Jesus' feet with her tears. Then she anointed them with a costly perfume —an act of great meaning in a day when men trudged over dusty trails in open sandals and looked forward to the restful cleansing of their feet when they entered a home.

> When the Pharisee who had invited him saw this, he said to himself, "If this man were really a prophet, he would know

who this woman is and what sort of person is touching him. He would have realized that she is a bad woman." Then Jesus spoke to him,

"Simon, there is something I want to say to you."

"Very well, master," he returned, "say it."

"Once upon a time, there were two men in debt to the same moneylender. One owed him fifty dollars and the other five. And since they were unable to pay, he generously canceled both of their debts. Now, which one of them do you suppose will love him more?"

"Well," returned Simon, "I suppose it will be the one who has been more generously treated."

"Exactly," replied Jesus, and then turning to the woman, he said to Simon:

"You can see this woman? I came into your house but you provided no water to wash my feet. But she has washed my feet with her tears and dried them with her hair. There was no warmth in your greeting, but she, from the moment I came in, has not stopped covering my feet with kisses. You gave me no oil for my head, but she has put perfume on my feet. That is why I tell you, Simon, that her sins, many as they are, are forgiven; for she has shown me so much love. But the man who has little to be forgiven has only a little love to give."

Then he said to her,

"Your sins are forgiven."

And the men at table with him began to say to themselves, "And who is this man, who even forgives sins?"

But Jesus said to the woman:

"It is your faith that has saved you. Go in peace" (Lk 7: 39-50).

It's important to remember this. Jesus meets us first with forgiveness. He tells us that He loves us—knowing full well what we are. We can't hide ourselves from Jesus, any more than the woman at that feast could. *And we have no need to!* Jesus lived and died to cancel our debt, to extend forgiveness.

The more we are aware of our need for forgiveness, the more quickly we'll respond to Him in love and faith.

It is, as Jesus said, faith that saves us—a wholehearted trust in Jesus as one who loves us as we are, and who is eager to reach out with forgiveness to cleanse our hearts and awaken love for Him.

"He who is forgiven much—loves much."

It's amazing, isn't it? Even our love for God depends on honestly facing ourselves, realizing our failures and needs, and trusting God's promise of forgiveness in Jesus.

"Your sins are forgiven."

Until you have heard those words and realized they were spoken to you, you're not qualified to be a teacher. You're not ready to communicate Jesus' love to your class. You can't even know that love yourself. The kind of faith the woman at the feast had must come first. God loves me as I am; in Jesus, He forgives.

## Living with forgiveness

Too many children and youth feel about Sunday school—and their teachers—as Naomi felt. "Everything was really phoney. They had nothing to offer me." A large part of the reason for these feelings is that so few teachers feel free to be real with their students. This was one thing Naomi was as a teacher. Real.

"When I taught, I admitted to my girls that this story had been hard for me to understand." "All of a sudden I realized that what I was doing was what Christ was telling His disciples He really hated! So I stopped right in the middle and told the kids that I felt I had really been unreasonable with Paul, and I asked them to pray for me. And they did."

Naomi decisively rejected the way of the Pharisee, and shared her real self, even her failures and needs, with her class.

There's something about forgiveness that frees us to be real with ourselves and with others. When Jesus comes to us with forgiving love, He both recognizes our sin and asserts our value. God *loves* us. Not because of what we *do,* or because of our goodness. God loves us because we are important to Him, so important that He planned His Son's Calvary death *for us.* However badly we have fallen short, however bitter or unloving we may be, however great our failures, Jesus' forgiving love insists that we are worthwhile and of infinite value to God. Your importance as a person does not depend on what you do for God, or on how good others think you are. *Your importance as a person is based squarely on the fact that God loves you.*

What this means in practice is that you and I don't have to pretend with people. Instead of pretending, we can open up our lives to God and let His forgiveness flow over us. We need to realize constantly that our sins are forgiven. And then, when we do, we'll begin to love. And love for God will overflow and change our lives. That love will be so real, it will carry, as a deep and flowing stream, others to Jesus.

Living as Naomi did, honestly, sharingly, revealing both her need for forgiveness and her love for Jesus, was utterly basic to her teaching success. By always counting on His love, by resting confidently in His forgiveness, and by showing that trust to her girls at times when she sensed a need for fresh forgiveness, Naomi helped them to discover who Jesus is and how much difference knowing Jesus makes in a person's life. And so can you.

## You, a unique teacher

I don't know you, personally, as you read these words. I don't know what you're like. I don't know your childhood, your present. I don't know the successes or failures you've known, the joys or tragedies that have helped shape you. I don't know if you feel confident or inadequate, if your satisfied or discouraged about your experience as a Christian and as a teacher.

I don't know you, for you are unique.

You're a distinct individual, like Peter or James or John or Naomi, who brings to your teaching ministry a personality all your own, with both weaknesses and strengths.

But I do know this, *whoever you are, God can use you to communicate His love to others.* God can use you as a teacher. You can have a tremendous impact on the lives—and eternity—of those you teach.

But you can only have this impact if, you've first of all, come to know Jesus' forgiving love. No Pharisees can qualify, nor anyone who has spent his life trying to establish his own righteousness, covering up his sins and failings, and awkwardly holding God at arms' length, lest He force him to stop pretending. The Pharisee was the one person who could never accept Jesus' kind of love or respond to it. And so the Pharisee could never know God, much less teach others about Him.

But if you've seen Jesus as He is, God's Son, eager to cleanse and free you from sin's bondage through His forgiveness, and if you've opened up your life to Him for that forgiveness, then you *can* teach, for you know Him and can share Him with others.

Sometimes, though, even Christians forget to keep on living in God's forgiveness. If you have—if you've slipped into a Pharisee kind of life, pretending with your class and other Christians—your teaching will come over as "phoney." You won't seem "real," and what you say about Jesus will seem unreal too.

So we have to start here in thinking about you, the teacher. We have to start here because a teacher is, first of all, someone who has accepted Christ's forgiving love and who is going on to live out that forgiveness in growing love for Him.

## REACT

1. When was the last time some person dear to you was hurt by a fault or failure of yours and responded with a truly accepting, forgiving love? Jot down briefly a short description of the situation and how this made you feel.
2. Does it help to realize that God has always had to work through persons who are, in themselves, untrusting, unloving, critical, or angry? How is it possible for God to help others learn about Him from persons like this?

## ACT

1. Study Luke 18:9-14, and note the difference in attitude between the two men. How do they illustrate what I have to say in this chapter? Which of these two men are **you** most like?
2. What do you think your students think of you as a person? Are you "phoney" to them or "real"? What, specifically, makes you choose one or the other?
3. In view of the reasons you listed in answer to number 2 just above, how can you—and thus the Jesus you speak of—become more real to your class members?

# 3
Life on the Upswing

I started to read the story and to read the events before and after, and got very involved with the study. Through the Holy Spirit, the Lord showed me so clearly that this was the essence of God Himself. . . . That affected my whole life. . . .

It was so exciting to me that I had been able to communicate what I had learned and experienced.

Life for Naomi was on the upswing.

Naomi began her teaching ministry with a deep sense of awareness of her distance from God. And in a sense, this was good. She couldn't slip into that Pharisee pretending pattern of life we looked at in the last chapter. She knew, like Simon Peter, "Lord, I am a sinful man." But soon life began to change for Naomi. Realizing her need, she began to feel the healing touch of the great Physician.

## Forgiveness' transforming power

It's good to remember when we think of the forgiveness God offers us in Christ, that He offers us far more than this. It's true that we never grow beyond the need for forgiveness. As the Bible says, "If we refuse to admit that we are sinners, then we live in a world of illusion and truth becomes a stranger to us" (Jn 1:8). No, the Christian way of life is to remember always that we are sinners and to be quick to open up our lives in confession to God when sin expresses itself in our lives. For we have His promise, "If we freely admit that we have sinned, we find God utterly reliable and straightforward—he forgives our sins and makes us thoroughly clean from all that is evil" (1 Jn 1:8-9).

But this forgiveness has a transforming power. God's forgiveness isn't offered because we are helplessly trapped, condemned to failure by our tendency to sin. Christ's forgiveness is given to break us out of the trap. The Bible says, "I write these things to you to help you avoid sin" (1 Jn 2:1). God's goal in our lives is to transform our character and personality, to reshape them until they match His own Son's (Ro 8:29). The unloving person we talked about in the last chapter, the untrusting, the greedy, the selfish, has been chosen by God to be remolded until he expresses God's own love, God's own trustworthiness, God's own self-giving.

To be a teacher, then, you and I need both to experience

the fact that we are sinners and to know the transforming touch of God Himself.

What was it that turned Naomi's life around? Not to make her sinless—for that's impossible—but to help her discover the reality of God and know His hand on her life.

What was the turning point and touchstone of Naomi's new life? God's Word.

## "I started to read..."

J. B. Phillips' translation of the New Testament renders the opening words of John's gospel in what I feel is a very beautiful way. "At the beginning God expressed himself." God reached out to us, eager to have us know Him. God shared, revealing His thoughts, His attitudes, Himself.

We know, of course, that that verse is speaking about Jesus. The eternal Word of God, the Bible tells us, "became a human being and lived among us. We saw His splendor." (Jn 1:14).

It's clear from the rest of Scripture just how accurately Jesus revealed God—just how perfect an expression of the Father the Son is. Once when one of His disciples begged, "Show us the Father, Lord, and we will be satisfied," Jesus had to respond sadly, "Have I been such a long time with you, without your really knowing me Philip? The man who has seen me has seen the Father. How can you say, 'Show us the Father'?" (Jn 14:8-9). Jesus is *the* Word, the eternal self-expression of the Father. Jesus is God; and knowing Him, we know God.

But how exciting to see the Bible use this same term, "the Word," of Scripture itself. Not that Jesus and the Bible, or that God and the Bible, are one and the same. But that God has expressed and revealed Himself in language as well as in the Incarnation. God has shown us who He is, what He is like, has shared His thoughts, has communicated Himself to us— in this Book we teach.

How important is self-expression in developing *any* relationship? You and I can observe a person and note his actions. We can see what he *does*. But unless he talks to us, unless he explains his motives and feelings and what his actions mean to him, we will never know him. For years I cleaned our home, dusting and mopping and vacuuming, because my wife is allergic to house dust. I used to get up early and clean while the family slept, so the dust could settle. And then when my wife woke up, I'd take her out to tour the freshened rooms. To me this cleaning was an expression of love, and I was giving a love gift to her in every tour.

It was only years later that I discovered how terrible the tours were for her, for she felt each one was criticism for her failure to do what a "housewife" is supposed to do! It was only when I explained what my action meant to me, only when I expressed myself in *words,* that she could understand me and what I did.

It's really the same with God.

How do we know Him? We can see what He has done in history. We can look at our own lives and experiences and wonder what purpose God may have had in this or that. But it is only when we come to the Bible and hear His explanation of Himself that we can begin to know Him, that we can begin to see the person behind the actions.

Even God's greatest act of love and self-giving, the crucifixion of Christ, is meaningless without explanation. Was it a tragedy? An unbelievable miscarriage of justice? Another evidence of the sinfulness of men? An admission of the weakness of a God who could not save His own Son from a horrible death? No! Christ's death was a towering act of disciplined love. God planned His own pain from earliest eternity, for you and me. And reading in the Scripture God's revelation of the meaning of this act, knowing the costliness of His love and the expense of His forgiveness, I can only bow in amazement that He should die for *me.*

"At the beginning, God expressed himself."

In the Bible, God continues to express Himself.

So somehow then, the Bible becomes vital in turning our lives around. The Bible becomes the focal point of our meeting with God, person to person, face to face. And we need to come to God's Word to meet him. It was this that Naomi began to experience. "At that point I felt that if God was really there and really had supervised the writing of the Bible, there had to be a reason for that story. So I asked him as simply as I could to help me forget the whole past and show me just why this happened.

"I started to read the story, and to read the events before and after, and got very involved with the study. Through the Holy Spirit, the Lord showed me so clearly that this was the essence of God Himself, that He was trying to show His people His holiness and glory and that a relationship with Him had to be on a special level—that He is a holy God. And it had never been related to me like that. It had been, 'You touched the ark! So God is punishing you for disobeying.' That affected my whole life."

You see?

This is what the Bible is all about—and what God's Word is to be to everyone who teaches it; not a book of stories, not a book of dry information, but a book of truth, a book in which God expresses Himself to us and through which He, Himself seeks to affect our whole life.

## The Holy Spirit

The Bible's impact on our lives isn't an automatic or a "natural" thing. It's supernatural. The author, God the Holy Spirit, is living within the believer to help us hear Him when we read.

This isn't the place to go into an extended discussion of the Holy Spirit or His relationship to the Bible. It is important, though, to point out one or two vital considerations.

It doesn't take the Holy Spirit's help to enable us to master the content of Scripture. Any atheist who might set his mind to it could master content, learn all the stories, memorize verses, and give biblical evidence for orthodox doctrine. Learning *what* the Bible says does not necessarily require the Holy Spirit's enablement.

It's the same with teaching. We can tell stories in Sunday school. We can discuss Bible doctrines. And those we teach can listen—and learn. *But no one apart from the Holy Spirit can say "Jesus is Lord!"* (1 Co 12:3). No one apart from the Holy Spirit can penetrate beyond information to discover the Person who expresses Himself in it. Only the Holy Spirit takes the objective truths of Scripture and makes them real to us. Only the Holy Spirit can take the values and attitudes and way of life of God Himself, expressed in Scripture, and blend and mirror them in our personalities, progressively changing us to become more and more like Jesus.

It's this Holy Spirit work through Scripture that you and I need to seek in our teaching. *And it's this Holy Spirit work in our own lives through the Word that we need to experience as teachers.*

God has expressed Himself in Jesus Christ.
God has expressed Himself in Scripture.
God wants to express Himself in you.

## Our responsibility?

Teaching the Bible, then, isn't something we can approach mechanically. It isn't something we can think of only in terms of methods and materials, or fresh techniques or exciting storytelling. Teaching the Bible involves sharing what *we* are discovering of God in our own study of His Word. And sharing what we are experiencing of God as the Holy Spirit works in our lives.

So Naomi not only started her teaching ministry with a healthy awareness of who she was as a sinner; she started with a personal involvement in God's Word—an opening of her life to the Holy Spirit that He might work in her through the Word.

And this is vital for you, the teacher.

Words that fall from our lips unlived and unexperienced come across as shallow, as unreal. But the Word of God? Ah, how different, how vital, how *real* this is! *God expressed Himself!* As we experience this reality, as we discover the truth of His words as the Holy Spirit makes them part of our lives, we too will express *Him*.

## REACT

1. Are you experiencing God's transformation through the Word? Jot down a brief description of the latest thing He's said to you, your latest experience of His truth.
2. Do you know a person whose life expresses the reality of a growing relationship with God? What is this person like? How do others respond to him or her? Think for a moment: what would he or she be like as a teacher?

## ACT

1. There are no "three easy steps" to a relationship with God through His Word, like that Naomi describes. But her approach is basic and helpful for any teacher. Notice what was involved:
   a. " I asked God . . . to show me."
   b. "I started to read . . . and to read the events before and after, and got very involved with the study."
   c. "The Lord showed me."
   d. "I had been able to communicate what I had learned and experienced."

   How does this compare with your approach to lesson preparation?

2. Why not stop reading this book here and spend time preparing your next Sunday school lesson? Approach preparation as Naomi did. God **is** faithful, and He does express Himself in His Word.

# 4

## Called to Care

So many things started to happen. But the basic thing was that my whole motivation changed. I was no longer really concerned that Pastor Howard knew I was there every Sunday. I no longer cared about the pat on the back for teaching and all that, which had been extremely important to me before. My motivation was for learning. Experiencing became really Christ-centered, and I just had a totally different attitude toward those kids. I was so involved with them and concerned for them, and I **loved** them just like my own kids, really.

There are many motives for teaching. One person may teach out of a sense of responsibility. He feels he ought to support the ministries of the church or that children ought to know the Bible. He's noticed how hard it is for churches to enlist enough teachers, and so he dutifully shoulders his share of the responsibility.

Others teach out of friendship. The superintendent of a department is a good friend. When he or she shares, "I've tried everyone, and I just can't get a teacher for that one class. Won't you *please* help me out for a while?" Well, what can you do? So you say, "All right. For you, I'll do it. But only for a while."

Perhaps you teach because you've gotten started, and there never seems to be anyone to take your place. You're tired. You'd like to be in an adult class or have an extra hour at home on Sunday morning; but after you've been teaching for years, everyone seems to expect you to keep on. You mention quitting now and then and often sigh to the superintendent how much you need a rest. But whenever you do, everyone smiles and says, "Why, we couldn't get along without *you*. You're the best teacher we've got! Our Sunday school just wouldn't be the same without you."

And some feel as Naomi did. That pat on the back for teaching, the fact that the pastor and others know they are there, is important. For it is true that too often a person's spirituality and his relationship with God are measured by what he *does* in the church. Usually we view Sunday school teachers as members of the elite. And for some, the feeling that others look up to them or feel they're "good Christians" because of what they do for God (even though this is the grossest sort of pride!) is very important.

It was important to Naomi. Even when she felt far away from God—even while she was doubting and questioning—she wanted others to think of her as a faithful "teacher," who was there every Sunday morning, doing her duty. She wanted to be respected and appreciated, even if it meant pretending.

So many motives for teaching. A sense of responsibility, a feeling you *ought* to teach, an expression of friendship, a habit, a desire to be looked up to by others—so many motives, and all so far from the great passion of Jesus, the Master Teacher. All so far from the motivation a teacher of God's Word is expected and invited to share.

When we think of motivation, as when we analyze interpersonal relationships, two categories are very important. One category is that of *performance*. In this category we can put everything that we *do* to *gain* something else.

For instance, in Sunday school a second grader learns his memory verse word-perfect and even masters the extra verses suggested. When he comes to class, he eagerly rushes up to his teacher and quotes them, smiling delightedly when she expresses her approval. He *did* something (learned the verses) to *gain* something (his teacher's approval).

We see the principle operating in all kinds of situations. A high schooler works hard preparing for a final examination so his grades will be high enough for the college he's set his heart on. The middle management executive brings home briefcases full of papers and works all weekend so he'll be advanced to a better position with higher pay. A couple, eager to break into a particular group, invites members of that group over to dinner so that they'll be invited over in return.

You can think of many more examples. For this "norm of reciprocity," as some sociologists call it, dominates and determines most relationships in human society. "If I do this, he (or they) will do this." We *do* in order to *gain*.

Looking back over the motives for teaching that I've sketched, it's easy to see that these are *performance* motives. Teachers who teach for these reasons are *doing* something (teaching in Sunday school) in order to *gain* something that is important to them (whether it's the feeling of having discharged a duty, maintained a friendship, earned status as one of the "spiritual" members of the church, or whatever). Somehow these motives for teaching all turn back on oneself. Ultimately, if you teach from any of these motives, you are teaching—not for Christ and for others—but for yourself.

Put most bluntly, I suppose, we'd have to call all performance-based actions—all *doing* in order to *gain*—self-centered or selfish.

It's not that *all* doing to gain, that all self-centered motives are wrong. That high schooler *should* study hard to get good grades and possible entrance to the college he wants. This kind of self-interest is usually quite healthy. After all, God loves me and wants the best for me. So I should be concerned about what's best for me too. Self-love *isn't* sin in itself; for Jesus said, "Love your neighbor, as you love yourself." If love of neighbor is important to God, and we know it is, then love of self is too. For Jesus puts them both on the same level: *"as* you love yourself."

However, when we move from motives for things like studying hard or working hard, to motives for teaching God's Word, things seem to be very different. Here there seems to be something basically wrong about using our class for our gain. Here we are dealing with other people, people whom Jesus says we are to love. How can it be love, if we show up for class each Sunday and tell our Bible stories or teach our passages because we want others to think better of us? How can it be love, if what we really care about isn't the persons we teach but the feeling that we've done our duty?

Somehow, there's something terribly wrong if our Sunday school teaching is a *doing* to *gain*.

## "... as I have loved you"

Even the commandment to love others as you love yourself, which Jesus labeled as like the "first and great commandment" to love God, fails to express the motive for teaching that can be ours. Jesus went far beyond this when He gave His disciples a "new commandment," and so opened up the door to an entirely new relationship with others. "Love one another;" He told them, "as I have loved you" (John 13:34, KJV).

Before we can grasp the meaning of this new way of living with others, we need to ask, How does Jesus love us? Is it selfishly? Is it in a performance way, self-centered, doing in order to gain? And we're forced to answer "No!" Jesus' love is of an entirely different order. Jesus' love was *costly;* it involved doing even at personal *loss,* doing that *others* might gain. "For while we were yet sinners," the Bible says, "Christ died for us." Now, some might be willing to die for an especially good man, but He died for us *"while we were yet sinners"* (Ro 5:8, KJV). God's love fastens on us in spite of who we are and asserts that we are important to Him. God sent His Son, and Jesus gave Himself *for us.*

This kind of love shifts motivation and relationships to a totally new level, and this brings up the second category of motivation—the love of Christ. Action (doing) no longer flows from self-interest (for gain). Action (doing) becomes an expression of love (for others). We can call motivation and relationships that express this kind of caring *love-based,* or *affirming.* They focus on the other person and affirm, "You are important. I do for *your* benefit. I *do* as an affirmation that you count. I *do* because I love you and because Christ loves you too."

It's just this that Jesus means when He says to us, "Love one another; as I have loved you." It's just this that must be our motivation in teaching.

We teach because we love.

## Dimensions of love

It's important to stop and think about ways that a Jesus'

kind of love expresses itself. We see it, of course, in the gospel records of His life on earth with people, as well as in His cross. For instance,

> While he was in one of the towns, Jesus came upon a man who was a mass of leprosy. When the man saw Jesus he prostrated himself before him and begged,
> "If you want to, Lord, you can make me clean."
> Jesus stretched out his hand, placed it on the leper, saying: "Certainly I want to. Be clean!" (Lk 5:12-13).

This story has always touched me deeply. Lepers in Jesus' day were outcasts. Stricken with horrible, putrefying sores, they repelled all who met them. Not only were they ceremonially unclean (and thus literally untouchable by their fellow Israelites), they were social outcasts, often making "home" the tombs or dumps outside cities. They could only beg their bread from the healthy, who loathed their looks and smell, and wait in huddled loneliness out in the deserted fields to die.

And it was a man like this, "a mass of leprosy," that Jesus met. "Do You want to make me clean?" There could be no doubt of Jesus' answer. Stretching out His hand to place it on the leper, who with his disease in so advanced a state must not have known another human touch for years, Jesus practically and powerfully expressed His love.

The power was in His healing word. The practicality was in His touch.

Our ministry as teachers blends this same pair. We teach a Word that, as God's expression of Himself, has power to heal and change. And as teachers, we have the opportunity to express Jesus' love in ways that accompany and authenticate that Word.

Think for a moment of ways Naomi expressed love in her relationship with her class of girls. Her basic attitude toward those kids changed, and "I *loved* them just like my own kids, really."

For one thing, Naomi's focus in teaching shifted from giving biblical information to communicating. "I tried to communicate with the kids, instead of just telling stories." We'll look later on at what is involved in communicating with persons and how it's different from just "teaching." But it's important now to note that the teaching focus, just like the relationship base, shifts from the job to the person. Naomi felt the difference in her life. It's a difference we can all feel. Somehow our students become important to us as individuals, as persons whom we love.

Naomi's love for her students was reflected in a desire for two-way communication. She became frustrated when there wasn't enough time to let the kids talk and share, to get to know them. "I felt really terrible because they had no chance to express themselves or get acquainted with one another." Again, when love came, Naomi saw her class members as persons; she wanted to know them personally and have them know each other. Love does do this. When you love someone, you want to know him. You want to come closer.

Naomi's desire to know her students as persons prompted action. "I asked if I could just *try* taking the kids for the whole time—from when they came to church until their parents left. [The pastor's wife] tried hard to understand me, and I know it was hard for her." But Naomi persisted, even calling parents for permission. And finally receiving it, she spent all Sunday morning (not just the short Sunday school class time) with her girls.

Naomi went out of her way to provide special experiences that she felt her girls needed to grow as Christians. "One Christmas I felt very strongly that the kids should have *something* that would help them experience what Christmas really means. So I went in search of a project. . . . We had a day when all of us got together—the kids and I—and baked everything. We weren't going to go out and buy any food at all; we were going to make it all." It meant a great investment of time and trouble. But Naomi didn't see it that way. It was something her girls needed, and she loved them.

Oh yes, Naomi built individual relationships with her students. "So I called this girl in my class during the week, and I'd say, 'I know you're praying for Sue. How are things going?' and so on. . . . It drew Pam and me close together, even though she's not in my class anymore."

Love found practical expression in reaching out to become involved in the lives of her students. And this kind of love can never be mistaken or hidden—or counterfeited.

## Do I have to love?

This is a peculiar question, really, because it's deceptive. It can't be answered yes or no, and for very important reasons.

In one sense, of course, love is utterly basic—utterly essential. The Bible makes this so clear that it's unmistakeable.

> If I speak with the eloquence of men and of angels, but have no love, I become no more than blaring brass or crashing cymbal. If I have the gift of foretelling the future and hold in my mind not only all human knowledge but the very secrets of God, and if I also have that absolute faith which can move mountains, but have no love, I amount to nothing at all. If I dispose of all that I possess, yes, even if I give my own body to be burned, but have no love, I achieve precisely nothing (1 Co 13:1-3).

And so, clearly, we can say, "If I teach with utter faithfulness and accurately expound the Word of God but have no love? I achieve nothing!" So yes, we do have to have love. Without love, our ministry as teachers and our lives as persons, achieve precisely nothing. In the Sunday school a performance-motivated ministry (*doing* our teaching to *gain*) is utterly worthless.

So we do "have to" love.

Loving is part of what teaching must mean.

But on the other hand, the question "Do I have to love?" begs the issue. Too often what that questioner really means is, "Do I have to do all those things Naomi did? Do I have to ask for more time for my classes? Do I have to get together with them outside of class? Do I have to plan projects for them? Do I have to call them on the phone and get to know them as individuals? Do I have to visit their homes? *Is this part of the job?"*

And as soon as *that* question is asked, it's clear we're back to thinking in performance terms! We're back to thinking of what we are supposed to *do.*

But love thinks of the other *person.*

Love says, "How can I love and help *you?"*

So let's not make a mistake here.

Loving can't be summed up in a list of things to do or not to do. Loving is caring and acting out of concern. When we love others this way, love itself shapes our lives and expresses itself in unique, distinctive ways. A teacher who loves his students won't necessarily do the things Naomi did. But love *will* express itself.

Yet there is still one other problem with the question, Do I *have* to love? Often it's uttered in desperation, like the lawyer who tried to find a way out of the commitment to others Jesus called for when He said, "Love your neighbor." Desiring to justify himself for his failure to love, the lawyer asked, "But *who* is my neighbor?"

Sometimes a question like this is asked in search for a way out of an impossible task.

"Love one another;" Jesus said, "as I have loved you." And we look at ourselves, we see our lack of love, recognize our selfishness, and cry out, "Lord, I *can't!* I can't love others like You do. Do I *have* to love?"

And to this question, Jesus answers, "No."

No. We don't have to do what we can't do. We can't love as Jesus did.

"He knoweth our frame," the psalmist says, and "remembereth that we are dust" (Ps 103:14, KJV).

How good to realize we don't have to do what we can't do.

Jesus explained it in that same conversation with His disciples where He gave the command to love: "Apart from me," He told them, "ye can do nothing" (Jn 15:5, KJV).

This is why we don't have to love. Because we can't. Because apart from the working of Jesus Christ in our hearts, apart from his life filling and infusing us, we can do nothing.

And this is why in the last chapter we looked at life on the upswing, life seeking a closer relationship with Jesus and opening up to Him, so that His ability can replace our inability. So that His love can flow through us where we are unable to love by ourselves.

This is what our faith is, you know. A relationship with Christ. A relationship in which He touches and transforms us, so that through us He can touch others.

"The love of God," Romans 5:5 (KJV) says, "is shed abroad in our hearts." And this is why we don't *have* to love. Christ in us, as we live close to Him, loves through us.

"I died on the cross with Christ," Paul writes to the Galatians. "And my present life is not that of the old 'I' but the living Christ within me. The bodily life I now live, I live believing in the Son of God, who loved me and sacrificed himself for me" (2:20).

And this is exactly what it takes for you to be a teacher.

## REACT

1. What are **your** motivations for teaching? Are they **performance** motives or love motives?
2. Read over chapter 1 again, and look for ways that Naomi expressed her love for her

students. What insights into love does this give you?
3. Think about your own class for a moment. Do they know you love them? Have you opened your heart to them as persons? How do you communicate your love to them?

## ACT

1. If loving your class members seems hard, read over in John 15 the picture of the vine and the branches. Can you see yourself as a branch, in intimate union with Jesus, with His life, His vitality, flowing through you and bursting into fruit as love and concern for others? Study the passage closely and open your life to Him, asking Him to fill you with his love.
2. Ask God's guidance as to how He wants to express love for your students through you—now, this week, this next class.

# 5
## Called to Teach

There were several kids in the class who were totally indifferent to everything. "Oh, we've heard that story seventeen times"; you know, that sort of thing. So I stopped telling a Bible story just to tell a Bible story. I would read the story at home and really study it thoroughly and watch God and see if I could understand why He put the story in the Bible to start with, what was practical about this for our lives, and why He did what He did in the story. And I tried to communicate this to the kids, instead of just telling stories.

## Called to Teach

One reason that Naomi continued to grow in her ministry was that she quickly discovered the difference between "teaching" and *teaching*. This is something many Sunday school teachers never become aware of. It's particularly true of teachers who, as Naomi describes, ask, "What are we going to do for half an hour? The story is only ten minutes." Ten minutes is plenty for "teaching." But not for *teaching*.

I suppose I'd better explain myself and my use of the same word to mean very different things. Actually, I use "teaching" this way because I'm convinced that it can mean *several* different things—not just two.

For instance, let's say that I'm "teaching" the multiplication tables. You know pretty well what I mean. I'm getting the kids to memorize (although apparently they don't do this any more since new math) their times tables: two times two equals four; two times three equals six; two times four equals eight; and so on. In doing this kind of teaching, my real concern is to *cause a child to memorize*.

How about if I'm "teaching" American history? Usually in this kind of teaching, I want my students to learn *what* happened in their past and to understand something of the men and events that shaped our country and their heritage. I want *to give them information and to help them understand past events*.

If I'm "teaching" drivers' education, I'm in an entirely different realm. Here I may give information, but my greatest concern is to help my students develop skills (a feel for the car, a recognition of signs, ability to follow the rules of the road) that will help them become good and safe drivers. In this kind of teaching I want them *to develop the ability to drive*.

We call all of these activities (drilling for memorization, communicating information, and helping others develop skills) "teaching." And, if you want to take a minute, you could think of a half dozen other activities that we call "teaching" too.

So you can see why it's important, when we start thinking about teaching the Bible, to define very carefully what kind of teaching we mean. The Bible does say to go and teach. But what kind of teaching ministry is God calling for? Naomi intuitively seemed to know, and she rejected "just telling the Bible story" to begin "to communicate."

## What is Bible teaching?

Perhaps we can get at the kind of *teaching* we're called to in Sunday school by asking a rather foolish question. "What's the difference between teaching Greek mythology and teaching the Old or New Testament?"

Our first reaction probably is, the Bible is true! Greek myths are merely madeup, even immoral, stories about false gods and goddesses.

Certainly that's a right answer, but not a complete one.

Both the Bible and a book on mythology are "religious" books. Both contain stories about God or the gods, that are supposed to record their actions. Both communicate information, concepts, ideas, about the nature of God and of men. Surely, we rightly label one set of stories "true" and one "false." But if these books simply contain interesting information to be mastered, each one (whether true or false) could be taught the same way!

Many children have been taught the Bible in just the way we might teach mythology—they've been told stories and given interesting information with morals tacked on. No wonder "Oh, we've heard that story seventeen times!" To them the Bible is just a true storybook! When they've heard the story, when they know the information, that's all there is to it for them.

And of course, this is how any teacher who views his ministry as using ten minutes to "tell the story" treats the Bible—as just another storybook, different only because it's true.

But there are other differences between the Bible and a mythology book. Because the Bible is true, *and because "truth" in the biblical sense means something very special, we can never teach the Bible as "telling stories."*

I've already mentioned one unique difference that sets the Bible off from every other book. The Bible is God's self-expression—His revelation of Himself. When we read the true information communicated in the Bible, we also meet God as a person. We hear His Voice. (In the next chapter, we'll think more about what this means to us as teachers and as listening Christians.)

The other unique difference that we need to consider is that the Bible's truth is rooted in reality. That is, that what the Bible reveals about God and us, about time and eternity is "real." The stories in the Bible are not simply historically accurate; they illustrate the information about reality that the rest of the Bible provides. Why does God show us reality? It's simple. In order that, through faith, we might experience it!

For instance, in the last chapter I wrote about love as something which God supernaturally creates in our hearts as we reach out to others for Jesus' sake. In one sense, this *teaching* of Scripture is information about God and about us. A concept is communicated that we can grasp with our minds, and retell to others. But this *teaching* is far more than information. And God is not primarily concerned that we should know the texts which teach it. Instead, God tells us about this kind of love so that we might trust Him for it and experience it! God is far more concerned that we should have His love overflowing in our lives than that we should be able to theologically explain it.

This is what is peculiar about the Bible as truth sourced in reality. We know God's Word only when we personally experience what it says. So our *teaching* must be geared to helping students *experience* God's truth, not just know information about it.

In this sense, *teaching* the Bible is far more like "teaching" drivers' training than "teaching" multiplication tables or American history. The goal for which our *teaching* must be geared is that our students will grow in the ability to *live* God's Word. We can never be satisfied with mere mental mastery of Bible truth. We must always be concerned about experiencing it.

It's easier now to see why "teaching" Greek mythology and *teaching* the Bible are two totally different tasks. At best, we can only teach mythology as interesting stories, as information, or ideas, which may excite our curiosity but which will not have any important effect on our life.

At best, we can only teach the Bible as God's revelation of reality, a reality that we are called as God's children to trust so completely that we rest the full weight of our lives on doing what God says and shows us. Bible stories, Bible doctrine, Bible history, are all to have a decisive impact on our lives!

This is why we must differentiate between "teaching" and *teaching*. For there is a kind of "teaching" which is designed to communicate information, to tell stories. And there is *another* kind of *teaching* that is designed to have an impact on life.

## Truth and life

At this point, perhaps, we're tentatively ready to define your task as a teacher. Put simply, it is *to communicate God's Word as a reality we can experience.*

How, then, can we teach the Bible this way? What is involved? What does it mean to teach the Bible as reality?

The diagrams given on the following pages may help clarify what's involved. Each begins with the assumption that our students are whole persons and need to be communicated with as whole persons. Put another way, children, youths, and adults are not merely minds. The decisions they make in life, the choices that bring them from experience to experience, are not made solely on the basis of information. If people were computers, programmed by information alone, we would respond to information. But we aren't computers. There are many factors besides information that affect our behavior.

For instance, take a primary-aged child, a six-year-old who develops a very normal fear of the dark. When night comes, he's not about to go down that dark hallway to get his pajamas! You may tell him, "There's nothing down there to be afraid of." And he may nod in agreement! But he's still afraid to go. If you're a Christian parent, you're very likely to tell him, "But God is always with you. You don't have to be afraid." And again he'll nod. But the chances are he'll still be afraid. The information somehow hasn't changed his feelings or freed him to make the decision to go down that hall. His fears seem far more real than God.

So you can see why we have a problem. How do we communicate true information so that it seems *real*?

Figure 1 illustrates one approach to teaching, an approach which you can see I feel is totally inadequate. The chart shows the learner as a complex blend of ideas and understanding, of feelings and emotions, of values and choices. This inadequate approach to teaching (one practiced too often in Sunday schools!) is simply *to communicate biblical information,* hoping that somehow it will filter down to touch the emotions and feelings and to affect values and decisions. But simple information (whether it is about Greek mythology or the Bible) has little chance of coming over as reality. What seems real to a person is a blend of understanding and feelings and values and decisions which are *experienced*. The Bible may be accepted intellectually by our learners and still not be seen or experienced as reality. We must communicate truth *as* reality, not merely as true information.

```
BIBLE INFORMATION  →        UNDERSTANDING

                            FEELINGS
                            EMOTIONS

                            VALUES
                            DECISIONS
```

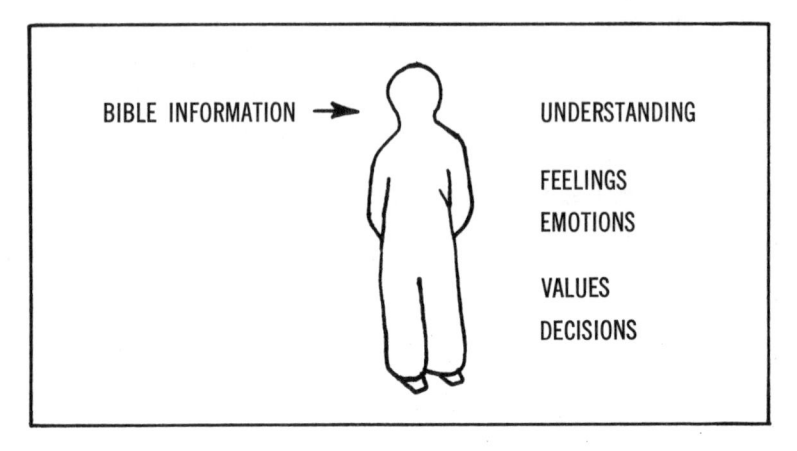

Fig. 1. Inadequate teaching seeks only to pass on Bible information.

Figure 2 indicates what we have to do if we are to communicate Bible truths as reality. We need to communicate them on each level of the learner's personality.

The teacher of the Bible, then, must not only communicate what the Bible says but also share what that truth means in terms of his or her feelings, values, and decisions.

We can see more of this process of sharing when we look again at Naomi's ministry. And when we see things like this:

"When I taught, I admitted to my girls that this story had been hard for me to understand. I had never admitted anything like that when I was teaching, but I just told them this had been a very difficult story for me to accept."

"I got there and started in on the lesson. It was a story on Christ's life, when He was expressing to His disciples that one of the most important things He desired from them was not sacrifice, but a whole new mental attitude. And all of a sudden I realized that what I was doing was what Christ told His disciples He really hated! So I stopped right in the middle and told the kids that I felt I had really been unreasonable with Paul, and I asked them to pray for me. And they did."

```
BIBLE INFORMATION  ⟼         UNDERSTANDING

FEELINGS         ⟼         FEELINGS
EMOTIONS                    EMOTIONS

VALUES           ⟼         VALUES
DECISIONS                   DECISIONS
```

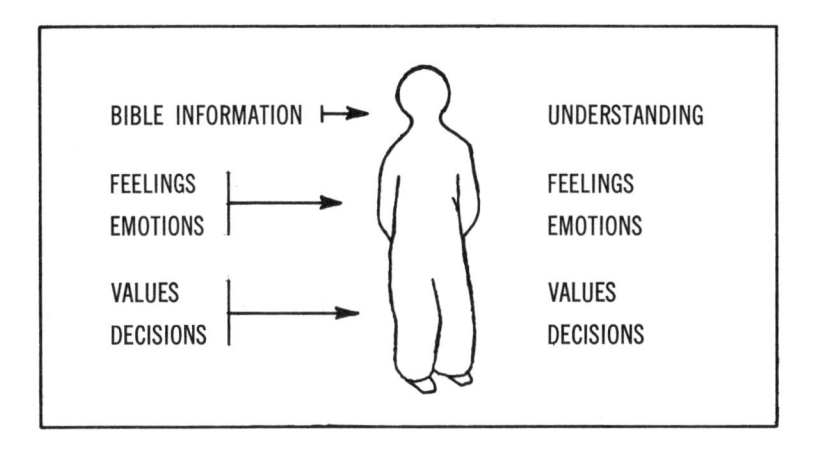

Fig. 2. Adequate teaching communicates feelings, emotions, values, and decisions *as well as* information.

When God answered the prayer about the hide-a-bed, "I was so excited I couldn't wait to get out. And I couldn't wait for Sunday morning. I was thrilled! I admitted to the kids that I hadn't really been very honest about it myself because I was trying to answer their prayer myself, and God just reached down and really answered it. And man, the kids—that's one thing they *did* go home and tell their parents."

## Sharing

The Bible says something very striking about sharing experiences that will help us understand what was so important about Naomi's sharing. Paul writes of God giving us "comfort in our trials so that we in turn may be able to give the same sort of strong sympathy to others in theirs." And he boils it down this way: "if we experience trouble we can pass on to you comfort and spiritual help; for if we ourselves have been comforted we know how to encourage you (2 Co 1:4, 6).

When we experience the reality of God in our life, we can share that reality with others.

But usually such sharing means sharing weakness as well. Why? Because we *are* weak. Because apart from Christ we can do nothing. Even the great apostle Paul didn't shrink from sharing his weaknesses with those he taught, even to admit,

> At that time we were completely overwhelmed; the burden was more than we could bear; in fact we told ourselves that this was the end. Yet we believe now that we had this experience of coming to the end of our tether that we might learn to trust, not in ourselves, but in God who can raise the dead (2 Co 1:8-9).

Now look back over these three quotes from Naomi's story.

Because she shared that it was hard for her to understand the story of the ark, when she told what God had showed her, the kids saw that she knew God as one who spoke to and taught her. Because she confessed her need when God convicted her, and asked their prayers, she communicated the reality both of her conviction by the Spirit, and the great importance she placed on being responsive and obedient to God. Because she shared how she had planned to answer their prayers herself, the children knew that God Himself had acted. Because they could see Naomi's feelings and emotions and her values and decisions as she sought to live by God's Word, they knew that everything she taught was real to her. They saw the reality of the Word in the life of the teacher!

And it is always to be this way.

No wonder Paul writes to Timothy, "Pay close attention to yourself and to your teaching" (1 Ti 4:16, Williams). Life and teaching are to harmonize so that the reality of the spoken word is mirrored in the experience of the teacher! No wonder the Bible says, to be an example for the believers "in your speech and behavior, in your love and faith and sincerity" (1 Ti 4:12). *Truth is communicated as reality when it is shared by those who are experiencing it.*

This does not mean, of course, that everything you share must be a sin or a failing. Of course not. Share the good things as well—the joys God gives you, the answered prayer, and victories. *Share whatever is real to you.*

But if you do this, there will be times when you must share failures. Because, you know, you and I are still sinners, still totally dependent on God and so terribly inadequate apart from Him.

So, be honest. Speak honestly of your feelings, your values, your choices, and how Christ speaks to you as you teach His Word to others.

Show them that the Bible is real by sharing how real it is to you.

## Communication

Communication, then, involves more than simply giving Bible information. For you, and for every teacher of God's Word, communication means *sharing.* Sharing your understanding of the Word you teach. Sharing your feelings as you experience God's dealings with you in your life. Sharing your values and your choices as you attempt to harmonize these with the Word. Sharing honestly and openly whatever is real to you.

With this in mind, then, we can take the next step in building our diagram of Bible teaching. As figure 3 shows, that next step is to add a *person*—you, the teacher.

Bible teaching is an *interpersonal transaction,* a sharing of what is being experienced of God's Word as well as what the Bible says.

You can teach Greek mythology as stories, without sharing anything of yourself. Greek mythology doesn't pretend to be reality.

But you cannot just teach the Bible as stories, as ideas and information. The Bible is a Book that reveals reality, that touches us in every human capacity. God's Word is to be understood, to be felt, to reshape our values, to guide our choices. So if you teach the Bible as the Bible must be taught,

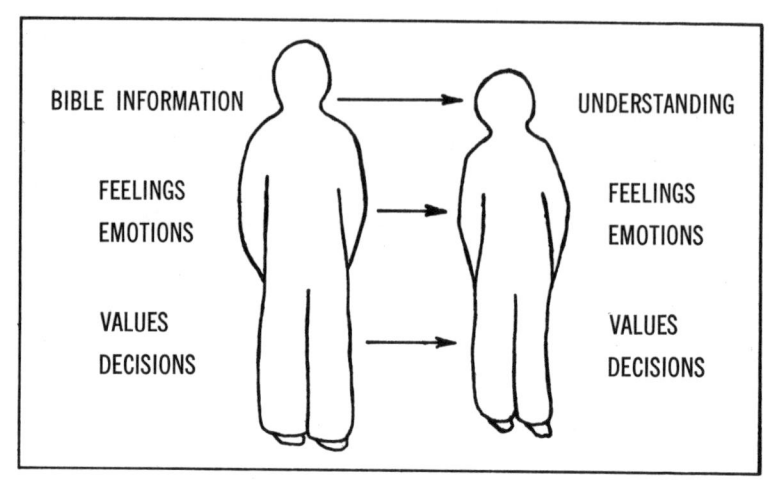

```
┌─────────────────────────────────────────────┐
│  BIBLE INFORMATION    →    UNDERSTANDING    │
│                                             │
│  FEELINGS             →    FEELINGS         │
│  EMOTIONS                  EMOTIONS         │
│                                             │
│  VALUES               →    VALUES           │
│  DECISIONS                 DECISIONS        │
└─────────────────────────────────────────────┘
```

Fig. 3

you must in the process share yourself. For it is through understanding, your feelings and emotions, your values, your decisions, *as you live the Word,* that your students will see God's truth as real and eagerly reach out to experience that truth for themselves.

## REACT

1. I have suggested that teaching the Bible is different from other kinds of teaching. Write down in your own words **why** Bible teaching is something unique.
2. Quickly read through the chapter again and check out what you have written. Did you catch the main points?

## ACT

1. Think back over the last class you taught. What kind of "teaching" was it? The kind of **information giving** that may be appropriate for teaching mythology but is not fitting for Bible teaching? Or **sharing,** that

communicates Bible truths as something **real to you?**

List briefly reasons why you feel your last class should fall into one category or the other.

2. Thinking over the last class, jot down ways that you could have made it **more** sharing. Remember, though, that for your teaching to be sharing, your preparation must be like that described on p. 43. You see, you have to be experiencing the truth you teach before you can share it. God's words must be **real to you** if you are to communicate them as reality.

# 6

Responding

I would read the story at home and really study it thoroughly and watch God and see if I could understand why He put the story in the Bible to start with, what was practical about this for our lives.

The kids responded way beyond my expectations. I felt there was something there, but I I was very shortsighted. And **they** taught me so much! In the story they would teach me things I wouldn't see; and in areas of personal living and daily activities and everything, they could relate God's sovereignty to things that were hard for me to have much faith about.

In the last chapter I developed a preliminary definition of your task as a teacher, and what it means for you to teach the Bible. According to that definition, your task is to communicate God's Word as a reality we can experience. Then we went on to see that you must be a *sharing* person—a person who communicates your own understanding, feelings, and choices as you live the truths you talk about.

This picture of teaching is true—as far as it goes. It simply isn't *complete*. A complete picture of teaching would show something happening *within the learner*.

Somehow we can't stop with the picture of you, the teacher, sharing. We must go on to your students, learning.

## What is learning?

There are as many different meanings for the word *learning*, as there are meanings for the word *teaching*. Look for a moment at the three illustrations I gave in the last chapter and note the correspondence.

| If teaching is— | the learning is— |
| --- | --- |
| causing to memorize the times tables, | memorizing the times tables. |
| giving information about past history, | mastering that information and demonstrating it on a test. |
| helping to develop driving skills, | being able to drive. |

But what is learning, if teaching is communicating God's Word as a reality that can be experienced? There can be only one answer. *Learning is experiencing Bible truths!*

This is exactly what Jesus taught in a well-known parable.

> "Everyone then who hears these words of mine and puts them into practice is like a sensible man who builds his house

on the rock. Down came the rain and up came the floods, while the winds blew and roared upon that house—and it did not fall because its foundations were on the rock.

"And everyone who hears these words of mine and does not follow them can be compared with a foolish man who built his house on the sand. Down came the rain and up came the floods, while the winds blew and battered that house till it collapsed, and fell with a great crash" (Mt 7: 24-27).

Every expression of God opens up our understanding of reality and is to be *put into practice*. Learning biblical information as one learns history or stories is totally inadequate. We are to hear the words of God and do them.

*This* is the learning that we as teachers of God's Word are to stimulate. Nothing else will do. We need to help our students grasp the meaning of Bible stories and truths; understand the implications of God's words for them as persons; and then act in faith to do the words of God, thus personally experiencing reality.

Understanding that your task as a Bible teacher is to help your students experience God's truth in distinction to simply knowing about it, will have a great impact on your teaching. For one thing, it will affect the *pattern* of the class. It will also sensitize you to certain things that must happen in a class session, if you are to lead your learners beyond information.

Study of teaching processes and how we guide students toward response, is so important that I've devoted an entire book to exploring it.* But *this* book is about you, the teacher. And I haven't space to go into specific methods that will help you accomplish what you must. Instead, for this book, I feel

---

* You may find it helpful to study that book *Creative Bible Teaching* (Chicago: Moody, 1970), to gain a clearer grasp of the *method* of Bible teaching. The book discusses the nature of Scripture, examines processes that need to take place in the classroom, and shows how to build your lesson to accomplish them. It also helps you master teaching methods that apply to each process, with separate sections for teachers of preschoolers, children, youth, and adults.

we need to focus on just what God has called you to accomplish in the lives of your learners, and what this means for you as a person. The focus is on you, the teacher.

## Learning

We've seen, then, that we need to gear our teaching for the practice of God's Word—the actual trusting response to what God says that necessarily involves acting on God's words. And we've seen that the first step in reaching this teaching-learning goal is *to communicate God's Word as a reality we can experience.* You accomplish this first step by a *sharing* kind of teaching, rather than a *telling* kind of teaching. You communicate feelings and values and choices as well as information and understanding. This kind of communication means that *you,* the teacher, *must also experience the reality of the truths you teach!*

The reason that we Bible teachers dare not "traffic in unlived truth" is that only when we are living and experiencing Bible truths can we share them as reality. Such sharing carries a compelling witness to your students. As you are real with them, the reality of God's Word is seen as the words are heard.

What else then needs to happen in the learner, before he will experience reality? And how can you, the teacher, work with the Holy Spirit to produce it? Figure 4 shows *barriers* between the various elements we looked at in the last chapter. Why barriers? Because, actually, they are there! *People do not automatically integrate their personalities.* In fact, it's common in our culture for ideas that are learned (and accepted!) to exist unlinked with a person's feelings and actions.

The other day in Sunday school, my youngest was wrestling and fooling around with a young friend, as his teacher tried to talk with the class. Later we talked the incident over with him. "Don't you *know* how impolite and disrespectful that is?" my wife asked, in more than a little horror. "I can't

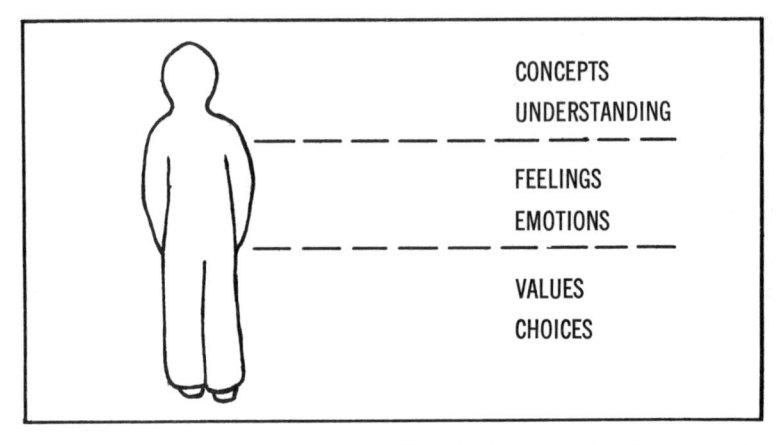

```
┌─────────────────────────────────────────┐
│                                         │
│     ╭─╮         CONCEPTS                │
│    ╱   ╲        UNDERSTANDING           │
│    │   │   ─ ─ ─ ─ ─ ─ ─ ─ ─            │
│   ╱     ╲       FEELINGS                │
│   │     │       EMOTIONS                │
│   │     │  ─ ─ ─ ─ ─ ─ ─ ─ ─            │
│   │     │       VALUES                  │
│   │     │       CHOICES                 │
│   ╱ ╲ ╱ ╲                               │
└─────────────────────────────────────────┘
```

Fig. 4. Because barriers exist in persons between knowing and feeling and doing, we need to help them break these barriers down.

believe you don't know that. You wouldn't start wrestling with him if we had company in our house, would you?" Certainly my youngest *knew*. But knowing did not, in that situation, so link up with his feelings and volition that it affected his behavior. He knew but didn't act on his knowledge.

This is perhaps the most serious thing we have to reckon with in communicating our faith. We know but do not act on it. We see this in adults as well as in children. What about the lady in your church who *knows* what the Bible says about gossip and control of the tongue but still spends much of her time gossiping about people? What about the couple who *knows* that marriage between Christians involves a lifelong commitment to one another, but who are both unwilling to work at their marriage and talk about finding "someone else."

In all our teaching of Scripture, we need to focus on breaking down the barriers—on linking God's Word with *all* of life. We need to help our learners, who have glimpsed reality in our lives, discover what that reality means for *their* lives.

## Responding

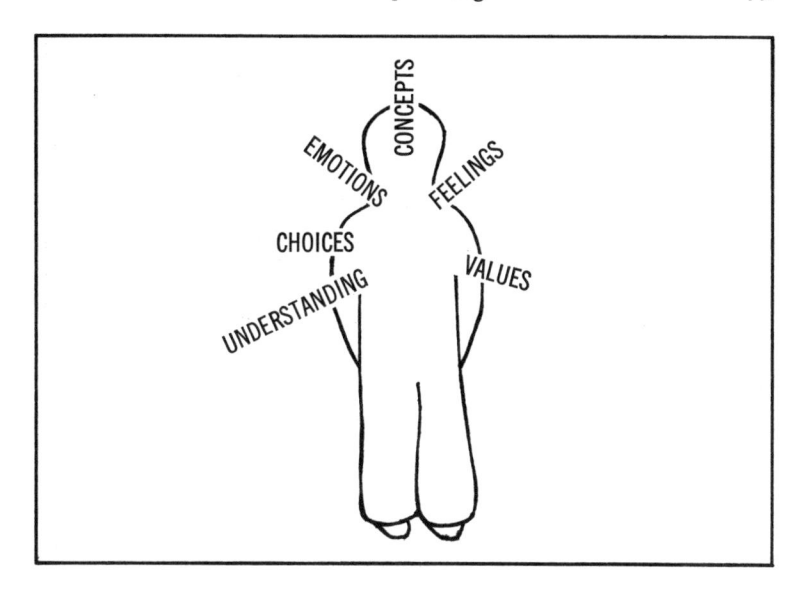

[Figure: outline of a person with labels CONCEPTS, EMOTIONS, FEELINGS, CHOICES, UNDERSTANDING, VALUES]

Fig. 5. Our lives are whole, the barriers broken down, when we are aware of the impact of truth on us as persons and when we go on to experience truth.

### Linked with life

We begin to break down the barriers between concepts and feelings and values by carefully exploring the linkage between these dimensions of life and Bible truths. We do as Naomi did by involving the kids in relating a Bible truth to "areas of personal living and daily activities and everything." *Linking with life is exploring the impact of God's words on our experience as persons.*

Yesterday I sat in on one son's Sunday school class. The teacher there worked very interestingly to link Bible truths with the children's lives. The lesson focused on what theologians would call the "omnipresence" of God. For the fourth graders, this was expressed simply as the fact that God is always with us. To help the kids feel the impact of this truth, the teacher first had each one go alone into a dark room and after a few minutes come out. Each went into the room again; but this time an adult they knew was there, and they talked for a few minutes in the dark. Then the children chose partners, and one was blindfolded. The blindfolded child was asked to find his way across the classroom, which was cluttered with chairs. After each had tried to go it alone, the first child was blindfolded again and this time led safely through the obstacles by his friend.

After these experiences, the kids sat down with the teacher to talk about them. When had they liked best being in the dark room? Was it easier to stumble blindfolded through the room, or did they feel more secure when someone led them?

Then, with their experiences discussed, each child moved around the room to read a number of Bible verses printed on oaktag sheets. Each verse spoke in some way of God's presence, God's protection, God being with His children. Each child chose a verse and brought it back to the circle, where they continued talking. This time each was asked to say why he had chosen the verse he did, and then later to describe a time when he had felt God's presence as the verse spoke of it. Class sharing ended with each of the kids and the teacher praying and thanking God for being with them and for caring for them as the Bible describes.

I know, of course, that not every class has the opportunity to move through experiences as this one did; not every class will be organized this way. I'm not even suggesting that this is "the" ideal approach to Sunday school teaching. But I do want you to note the way the teacher helped the children link their feelings, their past experiences, and real-life situations to the Bible truth. Too often "God is with me" is a meaningless phrase children have heard at home and at church. For the kids in this class, though, "God is with me" was no longer just words; it had been linked by the teacher with their feelings, with their choices, and with their experiences. The teacher had taken steps to link Bible concepts with life.†

It's important primarily to realize that this kind of linking requires that the learner *talk*. That the learner be involved verbally, thinking about his life, talking about his feelings and his experiences, discussing choices and values. Students of different ages participate to different depths. But don't forget that Naomi's class was made up of second graders! The ability they developed to see the relationship of Bible truths to "areas of personal living and daily activities and everything" was something that was "way beyond my expectations." Children *can* link truth and life when they are taught to. And linking Bible learning to life means that you, the teacher, need to invite your class members to share and talk over the meaning of the truths you teach them.

If you are going to teach the Bible as it must be taught, you, teacher, cannot do all of the talking!

## Going beyond

Linking truth to life, integrating all aspects of a personality around Scripture's revelation of reality is an important step in reaching our teaching goal. If we want our class members to learn the biblical way, so that they actually experience Bible truths, we do have to involve them in exploring with us the meaning for life of each truth we teach. This interactive process, this talking together about the meaning of Bible truths, is something we'll examine more closely in the next chapter as we see what goes on "around the table."

But discussion of the meaning of truth, so that our students are aware of the emotional and value impact of truths as well as of the concepts, still is not enough. We need to go beyond understanding to motivate a faith response.

In the last analysis, of course, motivating such a response is

---

† In my book, *Creative Bible Teaching,* pp. 115-126, you'll find many suggestions on how to link Bible concepts with the lives of learners.

the work of the Holy Spirit. It really is true that apart from Christ we can do nothing. We cannot respond in faith apart from His work in our lives. We cannot love unless He creates the love within us. And our students will not be able to step out by faith to experience God's truth, apart from the Holy Spirit's work of exciting and quickening that faith.

At the same time, the Bible does show us the *means* that the Holy Spirit uses.

God uses the Bible to open our understanding and show us reality. God uses you, teacher, to share yourself, and in the sharing demonstrate just how real and solid and trustworthy the written Word is. "You are our epistles," Paul wrote to the Corinthians, "written in living flesh, known and read by all." So it is you that God uses to provide the most compelling evidence that His Word *is* reality.

God the Holy Spirit uses you to focus the thoughts of your students on life. In the teaching process, He works in the minds and hearts of those whom you involve in thinking through the meaning of truth for life, and He Himself convicts and illuminates.

So it's not surprising to discover that God the Holy Spirit also uses *you* to motivate learner response to His Word.

There are at least three dimensions of your motivating ministry. The first is that you motivate by love. The Bible constantly links obedience to God with love for God. "If you love me," Jesus said, "keep my commandments." And "The person who loves me, he it is that keeps my word." Love is the greatest of all possible motivations for response. This is one of the reasons why the love Naomi felt for her girls is so vital a dimension of teaching. For that love was Jesus' love. It wasn't *her* love; it was the love of Christ that the Holy Spirit was shedding abroad in her heart. And the girls felt, experienced, *knew* this love.

There's something very special in knowing the love of God. "We love him," the Bible says, "because he first loved us."

God's love comes first, and when we sense it, our love is awakened. In experiencing the love of God, we are freed by the Holy Spirit to love Him in return.

You can see, then, why one way God the Holy Spirit wants to use you in the lives of your class is by helping you love them. When they feel the love of God through you, they will be motivated by a return love to respond to Him!

Sometimes we mistake what's happening. "My students love me so," a teacher will say. "They want to learn (or memorize, do whatever) for me." And this is true. They do love you. But over and beyond that, they love because in you they see Jesus Christ. And as a teacher you are privileged to help them focus on Christ all the love you both feel, and respond together in loving obedience to Him.

A second dimension of motivation is your example. Paul said, "Follow me, as I follow Christ." And again, "Let me be your example in this, my brothers." Somehow seeing in another person the reality and meaning of God's truth provides a compelling motivation. Here too, it's not difficult to see why. Picture a child as winter dawns, looking out over a nearby lake. He badly wants to step out on it, to slide, to fall, to celebrate winter with ice play. But he hesitates. Is the ice thick enough? Will it hold him? Is it safe?

And then you come along. You're bigger than he is, heavier, stronger. And so while he hesitates on the shore, you cautiously test the ice for him. Gingerly at first, watching for cracks to appear, listening for the groan of strain, you edge out further, until finally, convinced of its safety, you relax and wave to him. "Come on. It's safe! See, it holds me!"

How important it is for a child, or youth, or adult, who stands hesitating at the shore of a life lived by the Word, to find someone else standing confidently upon it. "Come on. It's safe! See, God's Word *is* reality. It holds *me!*"

The power of example, the power of the shared life, is one of the Holy Spirit's most powerful means to motivate others to respond to God in faith, and step out in trust upon His Word.

And the third dimension? Prayer. Naomi knew this too. "We had really prayed about Sue together and trusted the Lord for this." In prayer, as you come to know your class members as individuals, as you discover their needs, as you see the shores on which they hesitate, you can continue to work with the Holy Spirit to move your students to respond. "Whatsoever ye shall ask in prayer, believing, ye shall receive" (Mt 21:22, KJV). This too is a reality that we can trust, and trusting, look up to God and ask Him to do a work in the lives of individuals that both you, the teacher, and God who called you, love.

## REACT

1. This chapter sketches several themes which will be developed more fully in the next two. But check over your understanding of the basics by jotting down answers to these two questions and then comparing them with what the chapter says.

    Why do students need to talk in class rather than just listen? How do you, the teacher, motivate your students to respond and practice what the Bible teaches?

2. Compare the class described on pages 79-81 with your last class. How is it like and unlike what you have been doing in teaching? What, if anything, do the differences and similarities indicate to you?

## ACT

1. For specific and thorough help on how to structure a class session to move from

*Responding*

Bible information to response, study my book, **Creative Bible Teaching.**

2. Begin now to prepare for your next class, focusing first on personal preparation. Then examine carefully the lesson plan provided in your materials. When are you going to involve your students in talking over the meaning of the truths taught for their lives? How are you going to help them link the the truths to life?

# 7
## Around the Table

We didn't have a whole "spiritual" hour and a half. We went outdoors and played together, and we did a lot of different things. Sometimes we made things, like on Father's Day. But the time the kids loved most was when we just sat in a circle to talk and really get acquainted and get into things pretty deeply.

## Around the Table

Perhaps you've run into a teacher who shared—who talked openly and honestly about his experiences and feelings—and yet seemed to have little impact on his class, who generated little interest.

This does happen.

And it's important to understand why, if we're going to see who you, the teacher, need to be in the class session. And how the classroom will reflect who you are when you're teaching.

To build that understanding, let's start with the following situation. You've just been on a fantastic trip to Hawaii. For years you've wanted to go there. You've examined brochures, tuned you TV to all the travel shows that showed it, read articles in travel magazines. And at last, the opportunity came. Two weeks! For two whole weeks you actually walked those fabled shores. You laid on the beach, you clambered up the sides of a volcano, you flew over and around the islands, you took a boat cruise around the coast, you did everything you'd read about. You experienced for yourself the reality of what you'd simply read about in the brochures.

And did you take pictures! Slides, movies, stills—everything.

Now you're home. You want to share this experience, which has been so exciting and wonderful for you. So bubbling over, you invite some friends over, set up your movie and slide projector, and *share*—for four hours! As you see the now familiar scenes on the screen, all your thoughts, all your feelings, are relived; and you honestly and openly express them to your friends.

All right. How do your friends respond? Are they excited? Are they convinced by your sharing? Have you reached *their* emotions, *their* values, by simply sharing yours?

No, of course not. You know what has happened as well as I do. You *bored* them!

Now, as strange as this may seem at first, the most excited teacher who is *personally* experiencing the reality of the Bible words he teaches, who eagerly and openly shares all with his class, may be totally boring!

## Why?

Well, why was our Hawaiian traveler boring? There are probably a number of reasons, but I think the most important are these. He is making the others sit still—for himself. He isn't concerned about their involvement or interest. Not really. He's only concerned about reliving his own experiences. He is using them.

This is true even if his motives are good. Even if he wants to motivate them to respond ("Come with me to Hawaii again next year!"), his motives don't come across. The captive audience still feels captive, still feels used, manipulated. And they are convinced that the one sharing doesn't care—not really—about *their* feelings, *their* interests, *their* ideas about Hawaii.

And what's more, they're right!

He doesn't care. Because if he was truly interested in them, he'd stop talking long enough to ask, "How do *you* feel about this?" or "What interests *you*?" or "What would *you* do—lie on the beach or take out a fishing boat?" If he were truly interested in them, *he would encourage them to share too.*

I think you get the point that I'm making.

If your sharing is to *communicate,* it needs to be in a context of interaction. If you're going to reach the feelings and values and volition of your learners, you have to love and care for each of them as individuals.

## Listening can show love

In an earlier chapter we looked at the change that took place in Naomi's teaching as she began to truly love her girls. At the end of that chapter, I asked you to look over Naomi's story and see what she did that showed love.

I hope you caught one of the most important ways—a basic

and, in fact, essential way. "Sometimes I'd start talking to them, and I could see that there were too many things bugging them from last week; so I'd forget the story, and we'd sit in a circle and talk about these things openly." Naomi was so concerned about her girls as persons that she took time to listen to them and to change her teaching approach to fit their needs and mood.

Bible teaching is an interactive process. That is, it is never best as a one-way kind of thing (like the Hawaiian traveler's telling of Hawaii. Even the use of visual aids didn't keep this from becoming boring!). There are a number of reasons for interaction that we'll look at in this chapter. But the need of each student to sense God's love for and interest in him as a person through the teacher's Christ-generated love is an overriding one. When a student experiences such love and interest, and is invited to share himself, then the teacher's sharing communicates. When sharing is not *mutual,* when teacher and student are not both involved in expressing their lives, then sharing by the teacher alone becomes boring and soon loses its impact.

How do you encourage the students to share? How do you develop a climate for mutual sharing? Probably the most crucial issue is this: *Do you love the students enough to want to know what they think and feel?* And the second is, *Do you know how to express that love in listening?*

In another book, I've written about the kind of listening that communicates love and encourages sharing. Here are a few thoughts from it:

> Often we don't truly listen to others. You've seen people taking part in conversations like this. One person is talking, but no one else is listening. Everyone is just waiting for that person to stop talking so he can start in.
>
> At times like these we're usually thinking more about what we plan to say next than about what the other person is say-

ing. Our eyes wander, we open our mouths at the slightest pause in the other person's stream of words, we seem agitated and eager to have our turn to speak.

When we're acting like this, our lack of concern for the other person is communicated—loud and clear. We don't really care about him; we simply have made a bargain with him. We'll let him talk at us if he'll let us talk at him. Neither of us has to communicate or come closer. Neither wants to, and neither does.

No, listening that says "I'm interested and willing to come closer" is the kind of listening that communicates caring. It's not worrying about what I plan to say next, but trying honestly to understand what the other person is saying now. I may not understand. I may miss the point. But if I'm really trying to understand, that other person will sense it and will recognize the fact that I'm holding open the door of friendship.

*Listen for feelings.* . . . If we resist listening only to the idea a person expresses, we can begin to hear some of the feelings. When we listen for feelings, we get a better idea of what a person is really trying to communicate. For instance, Carol was one high schooler who responded to a question I asked about her friendships. Carol uses words here that express ideas, but everything she says indicates that underneath are some very deep and important feelings. If she said these words to you, what feelings might you think she was trying to share?

> It seems that I have a lot of friends, but hardly any real or close ones. They are nice but at times distant or spiteful, or they are nice to me but talk about me. Even the kids I consider to be close friends at times seem to look down on me.

The feelings come out, don't they?

And when we listen for them, we hear them.

Of course, we may misunderstand the feelings we think we hear. Then our listening can lead to *reflecting,* to throwing back what we think we've heard for our friend to check out for us. A reflecting response to Carol that says I want to understand what she's saying might be, "You feel uncertain about how your friends feel about you?" Or, "You don't feel you can trust your friends, then?" Responses like these show that we're trying to understand what is really important to the other person; that we don't care about abstract ideas, but about *her*. And that we care enough to be sensitive to how she feels.

*Response with self-revelation.* [A sharing] relationship means that we must give as well as receive. This is where self-revelation fits in.

When we respond to another person by revealing something of ourselves—right down on that "feeling" level where we live—we tell them we're willing to give.

This is vitally important—to let another person know that in our relationship with him we don't expect him to do all the giving. How do we tell someone that?

By not only trying to understand their feelings and experiences, but sharing ours in return. "It's a pretty awful feeling, that others don't respect you." This kind of response to Carol would show that you want to understand. But to share similar feelings that you've had tells that you are willing to *give* \*

I've quoted these extended passages, first of all, to show something of the importance of listening to others and also to show the *kind* of listening that communicates love. The link between listening and sharing is *responsive* sharing, that is, sharing that ties in with feelings or experiences the other person expresses. Or, if you introduce a topic (which is usually the case in teaching) sharing that invites a response. "When have you felt like this?" "Does this problem ever crop up in your life too?" "What has helped you in this area?"

In teaching, as in conversation, listening with love and honest interest establishes a climate for mutual sharing. And

---

\* Larry Richards, *How Do I Fit In?* (Chicago: Moody, 1970) pp. 27-30.

this climate of *mutual* sharing is vital; in it, understandings and feelings and values and choices that you seek to communicate to your students are *heard*.

## But what about the lesson?

It's easy to misunderstand what I've been saying in this chapter and to feel that I am proposing a contentless, Bible-less discussion about whatever your students want to talk over at the moment.

This isn't what I'm suggesting at all.

Instead, I'm saying that the teacher who comes into the class and does all (or most) of the talking about Scripture and his experiences, will *not* communicate the Word to his students as reality or motivate them to experience it.

Several processes need to take place in classroom learning. It may help to see how listening and mutual sharing fit into your class if I outline these processes. I've given each an easy-to-remember (though peculiar) title.†

*Hook* is the first process. It's a process designed to gain the attention and interest of the learners and to lead them into the Bible for God's point of view, by raising an issue that is important to them. This last point is important. What God says *is* important to each of us, but we need to *feel* its importance. Whenever you teach any passage of Scripture, you need to ask, How is this truth important to my class members? To me? How will this affect their lives and mine? When you've asked these questions, you know how to "hook" your students. *You involve them in an exploration of the very aspect of their lives that the truth to be studied will affect.*

Notice that already we're in an interactive setting. Already, by involving students in exploring a part of their lives and experience, we're in the realm of talking things over, of listening, of mutual sharing.

† These processes are discussed more thoroughly in *Creative Bible Teaching,* pp. 108-113.

## Around the Table

For this first process in the well-structured class, you, teacher, need to be a person who is interested in your students' thoughts and feelings and experiences, the kind of person who communicates that concern by listening and by sharing too.

*Book* is what I've called the second process. What it involves, of course, is moving into the Scripture to see what God says about the experiences and feelings we've discussed. God's Word is truth and does reveal reality as we are to experience it. So it's crucial for you and your class to come to an accurate understanding of God's revelation. In this process, then, depending on the age and background of your students, you either tell them a Bible story, explain what the Bible teaches, or lead them in direct Bible study to find out for themselves.

*Look,* the third process, is one in which you move from Scripture back to the present experience of your students, to explore with them the meaning of what God reveals for their lives. Note that here too, listening and sharing are vital. Only as your students honestly talk over the situations they find themselves in can they apply what God says to individual needs and problems, your own as well as theirs. Christ's pattern for Bible study is "hear and *do*." We need to understand what we hear; but we also must define what we are to do, so that we might respond in faith and practice the Word.

The final process, I've called *Took.* Like a vaccination, the Bible is not really helpful until it has "taken," until it is actually being implemented in our lives.

While there may be little one can do *in class* to ensure a student's acting on God's Word after class is over, what one *can* do in class (principally in sharing the reality of God's Word as you are experiencing it yourself, and encouraging learners to act on what God says) is again best done in the interactive, mutual sharing context.

In short, *three of the four basic teaching-learning processes that operate in the classroom require interaction, and all four are strengthened by it!*

So you can see that by saying you, the teacher, must listen as well as share, and may even at times feel the need to set aside the day's lesson just to talk, is *not* suggesting contentless or Bibleless teaching. Not at all. It's saying that for the Bible to permeate the lives of the learners rather than to merely be accepted as information, a context of mutual sharing needs to be developed, and the teacher needs both to listen and to share.

We can now state some additional reasons why Bible teaching is to be a two-way, interactive process, rather than a one-way "telling." First, you recall, I said that we need to have a two-way, interactive relationship in class because listening to students communicates love. Second, I suggested that listening on our part gains us a hearing when we speak. Our students will hear our sharing much more eagerly when we show interest in what they have to share too. And there are additional reasons for making sure that what happens in the classroom is interactive.

## Interaction relates and reveals

Have you ever noticed how hard it is sometimes when you read a portion of Scripture to see how this applies to your life? At times you may see the application the Holy Spirit has for you immediately; at other times, nothing.

It is always hard to move from Scripture to an examination of our lives and to discover the many ways God's truth may affect us. Part of the reason may be that we're not used to studying the Bible this way. Part of it may be that many aspects of our personalities and our lives are hidden from us. At times we simply "don't see" something that to another person seems striking and clear.

These things point up the advantage that studying the Bible with others gives us. If *we* don't see an application, another person in class may! If we haven't thought of a particular experience or need in relationship to the passage we're studying, someone else may. As one person reveals how the Word of God speaks to him, we may discover a fresh way the Word speaks to us!

It's this phenomenon, that when several people explore something together, greater understanding and insight are generated, that makes sharing so important when we study the Bible. The more our students contribute, the more varied the applications of a truth that we see, and the more we open up our lives to the probing of the Holy Spirit and look to Him for personal direction and guidance. Figure 6 shows what happens when a Bible passage has been studied and a principle or truth discovered. The class then shares together how this truth may affect their lives and how they may respond and put it into practice. The more the members share, the

Fig. 6

| Principle | Varied application | Examination of sensitive area | Personal decision |
|---|---|---|---|
| Joy in sacrificing self for others | by listening<br>by visiting sick<br>by helping sick<br>by shopping for sick<br>by baby-sitting<br>by cleaning<br>by having people over<br>by giving up best ← place or best job<br>by putting another first | How do we compete for first place, rather than give?<br>Why?<br>in church ←<br>at home<br>on job<br>etc. | I will try this week to . . . |

greater the application possibilities are seen to be. And then together you examine areas of particular or personal need. Finally, in view of the response possibilities explored, each can seek God's direction in how he is to respond and do the Word.

Interaction, honest sharing and exploring of our lives with others when we meet as a class, helps us discover the meaning of the Word for our lives and motivates response. So interaction is important for *relating the Bible to life*.

The final thing to note here about an interaction kind of class is that when you do involve your students in talking and sharing, they reveal their needs to you and to each other. This means a lot to you, the teacher. It means you know how to pray for them. It means you know what truths of Scripture they may need to grasp and apply next. It means you know how they think and feel and choose; and so in your own sharing you can speak directly to their minds and emotions and values, not shooting in the dark, but ministering to each individual as a person whom you know as well as love.

And never underestimate the importance of knowing your learners' needs. This alone can transform your ministry.

So interaction around that classroom table *is* vital. When you invite your students to talk and to share rather than dominating the class with your talking and sharing, you show love and personal concern in ways they will feel. You gain a hearing for what you do share. You help them discover how God's Word speaks to our lives. And you come to know each student as an individual, with needs that you can move to meet through prayer and personal involvement.

## REACT

1. I have sketched what happens in a class as a conversation between students and teacher focuses on the Bible. In thinking about

your own classes, which would you say they are most like:

    Showing slides and talking of Hawaii?

**or**

    A conversation focused around Scripture?

2. For a detailed explanation of what happens in the classroom and how you build a lesson that **both** encourages interaction **and** keeps the focus on Scripture, read **Creative Bible Teaching.** As noted, it contains help for teachers for every age level, from preschoolers through adults.

## ACT

1. Do you believe your students see you as a person who loves them, listens to them, and wants to understand them as well as share with them? Check to see just how much you know about them as persons: write the name of each student on a sheet of paper, and then jot down **everything** you know about him—including things like his feelings, interests, problems, relationships with God, parents, friends, and so on.

   You should be able to tell very quickly if you have been truly focusing on your students as individuals.

2. Many times teachers do not develop the kind of in-class climate written of in this chapter because they have felt their job is to tell only what the Bible says. From what you've read in this book so far, how do you now view your role as a teacher? Take time to write out who you, a teacher, are, and how you are to conduct your ministry. (Review earlier chapters if you wish.)

# 8
## Stepping Beyond

And I said, "Well, my real reason for teaching Sunday school is to communicate to **you** how to communicate to **her.** I want you to experience how neat it is to really tell people about the Lord and just have it be your whole life, not a separate thing on Sunday."

So I called this girl in my class during the week, and I'd say, "I know you're praying for Sue. How are things going?" and so on. We did invite her to parties, and she did come to Sunday school a couple of times. I promised Pam, "If you bring her, I won't embarrass her and I won't embarrass you."

Graduation was in the spring, and the girl in my class, Pam, went into high school, and Sue was still just as far from the Lord as ever. Once in a while when I'd see Pam around church, I'd say, "How's Sue?" and she'd say, "Well, she's moving back East." Well, finally, she got Sue to go to camp, and she met the Lord. After the sermon (it was the day Mr. Richards preached in church), I saw Pam and Sue and went back to say hello; and Pam said, "Oh, guess what. Sue met the Lord!" And I just went to pieces.

In the last chapter I looked at you, the teacher, in the classroom. I suggested that you need to develop an interactive, sharing climate, where you all listen to one another and share with one another. This climate, it seems to me, is crucial if you are to communicate truth as experienceable reality and if you are going to lead your class members to examine their lives in the light of Scripture. All this is truly basic to guiding learners to personal response to God's truth, to that doing of God's Word which Christ presents as the only appropriate response when we hear what He has to say. But while basic, even the best in-class climate and process is inadequate for fully motivating response. Somehow you, the teacher, need to go a step beyond.

Several things that Naomi shared, and some things I know about her aside from what she told me, indicate the direction her steps beyond the classroom took her and her classes of primary and junior high girls. And we need to explore them—not as a demand that you do exactly the same things with your students, but rather to open up awareness of possible ministries God may invite you to experience and *enable* you to experience, as His love moves you. We do need to explore them, for too often teachers in Sunday school have been led to see their ministries simply as a one-hour-on-Sunday-plus-preparation kind of thing, rather than a doorway through which they (and Christ) might enter others' lives.

If you, the teacher, truly do want to touch your students for Christ, Naomi's experiences give some excellent guidelines for stepping out beyond the classroom into learners' lives.

## Be with them.

There were many ways that Naomi did God's truth and invited her girls to be with her in the doing.

Often, of course, she was simply with them as a person, as when part of her hour-and-a-half Sundays was spent in play. Primary girls, young second graders, know play as a large part of their lives. And so Naomi played with them, to share this part of their lives, and in the sharing, to communicate love.

Sundays didn't provide much time for doing fun things together, though. So Naomi went beyond. She told me that as God was changing her attitudes and her teaching, the conviction grew that she just had to get to know the girls better than she did. So she determined that she would set aside one day a month to be with them, one whole day to go to a zoo, to have a picnic, to have them over to her house, to be together.

This wasn't easy for a mother with three children, who works part time as a buyer in her husband's business—a busy person, like you and me. But it was important to Naomi to be with her girls.

Being with them helped her to know each girl as an individual, to discover needs as she saw how they played together and how they talked about their homes and schools and friends. Being with them helped the girls know Naomi too—to know her as a real person and sense the reality of her love for them (and through her love, the love of Jesus). But Naomi didn't want to be with them *just* for this. Naomi wanted to help them respond with growing trust and obedience to Jesus.

### Do with them.

One thing Naomi reports illustrates very clearly the principle of motivating learners to respond to God by you yourself *doing,* while they are with you. It's the story of the Carascious family.

"One Christmas, I felt very strongly that the kids should have *something* that would help them experience what Christmas really means. So I went in search of a project." She searched for just the family the Lord wanted her and the girls to become involved with and had difficulty finding them. "So the parents started telling me, 'Why don't you just collect money from the kids and *you* take it down there?' And I said, 'That's exactly what I *don't* want to do!' " Naomi wanted her kids to become *involved* in showing Christ's love personally, not impersonally through contact with cash instead of persons.

As Naomi shared the process she went through in locating the family, in speaking with Mrs. Carascious, in being rebuked by her, in explaining Mrs. C.'s feelings to her class, in working with the kids on the selection of gifts, in baking the food they brought with them, and in loading the camper full of girls and gifts, it's very clear that it was Naomi who "did" the project. She had to spend hours and hours in preparation, in visiting, in shopping, in phoning, and talking. But in every way she could, Naomi involved her girls so that they were *with* her as she sought to show and share Jesus' love in a practical way, to give as an expression of thanksgiving to God for His own unspeakable gift to us.

My wife's mother is a wonderful German cook, who prepares all the traditional dinners with great skill. But as my wife grew up, her mother couldn't quite stand the presence of a useless little girl in the kitchen. It was so much easier just to do it herself and do it right. So when it came time to prepare dinner, little Martha was shooed out of the kitchen, out of the way. And you know the result. Nineteen-year-old Martha, when I married her, couldn't cook! Her mother's *ability to do* was never communicated, never developed in her.

I think the analogy is all too clear. Often the living faith of adults, of parents, of teachers, of grown-ups in the church, is lost to growing generations because we do not let them *be with* us we live our faith in Christ, as we *do*.

Naomi refused to make this tragic mistake. Instead, with the Carascious family and in many other ways, Naomi sought ways to live her faith, and to involve her girls with her.

With younger age groups, this providing opportunities for

our students to be with us as we do may be the most we can do in motivating personal response to God. But being with, participating, sharing in living for Jesus Christ, is a most powerful motivating force. And certainly it is a foundational way to go beyond the classroom to lead our learners into living for and with the Lord.

## They do, as you are with them.

When Naomi began to teach junior high girls, she began working with young people who have a real capability to respond to Jesus and to express their faith in obedient action. To move her girls toward this kind of life, Naomi again invested her life with them. She led them into sharing in class, into mutual exploration of God's Word. She spent extra time to be with them in fun things as well as Sunday mornings. She looked for ways to have them with her as she expressed her faith in Christ in obedient action.

Now with the junior highs she took them a step further—a step illustrated in the quote at the beginning of this chapter. "My real reason for teaching Sunday school," she told Pam, "is to communicate to *you* how to communicate to *her*." Naomi's goal was that her *students* might do.

Here, though, Naomi had a problem. It would be most effective if she could be right there, standing by their side, as they stepped out to live for Jesus. Just as learning how to cook moves from being with Mom and watching her as she cooks, to Mom watching as her daughter cooks, ready to give suggestions and support when needed. Or just as when a student pilot takes up the plane with his instructor in the back cockpit. He doesn't solo the *first* time he flies the plane himself. He solos only after he's flown the plane a number of times with the instructor there.

Motivating a *doing* faith is much like this. Ideally, the one who knows how to obey and respond to God is by the side of the one who is learning to do as long as he's needed for suggestions and support.

But Naomi couldn't go into the eighth grade with Pam and sit beside her as she talked with Sue. Naomi couldn't walk home with the girls, listen to their chatter, sympathize as Sue talked of her parents' coming divorce. Naomi couldn't be physically present with Pam as Pam tried to share Christ and love Sue. But Naomi could show that she really was "with" Pam in Pam's *concern* for Sue.

How was Naomi "with" Pam, as Pam responded to do God's Word? "So I called this girl in my class during the week, and I'd say, 'I know you're praying for Sue. How are things going?' and so on. . . . Once in a while [after Pam went into high school] when I'd see Pam around church, I'd say, 'How's Sue?'. . . I saw Pam and Sue and went back to say hello; and Pam said, 'Oh, guess what. Sue met the Lord!' and I just went to pieces."

Later Naomi talked of their relationship, and said, "What was really neat about it was that Pam and I had really become close friends. And we had really prayed about Sue together even though she's not in my class anymore."

You see how Naomi was constantly "with" Pam?

Not physically. Of course not. But knowing Pam's concern for Sue and her desire to see Sue come to Christ, Naomi let Pam know constantly that she wasn't alone, that Naomi was truly "with" her. Naomi called, to ask about Sue and to encourage Pam to keep praying. Naomi maintained the contact and concern even after Pam left her class, just by saying, "How's Sue?" Naomi developed a close relationship with Pam as they prayed together and trusted the Lord for Sue. In attitude, in concern, in every way, Naomi *was* with Pam, supporting and helping and encouraging and saying, "I care."

What are the needs of kids in your class, teacher? What are they concerned about? How do they need to step out to do the words of God in obedience to Jesus Christ? Knowing the needs and concerns of your students, you can motivate response by being with them and letting each know that you are with *him*.

There is something tragic about young people or adults who are told in Sunday school what they must do to live God's Word, but who are not shown that others care about them and are with them as they seek to live for Jesus. We need each other to be with us, to support us, to care, to encourage us to respond to God. And you can be used by God to help your students become doers instead of hearers, as you show them that, as their teacher, you truly are with them.

## Accountability

Naomi's relationship with Pam illustrates another aspect of motivating response to God's Word, which we will call "accountability."

Most simply put, accountability is expecting a person to respond and demonstrating this by checking up on him.

In a very real sense, holding a person accountable is a true ministry. It shows that you really *care* whether he is growing or not, that you care whether he follows through on what the Word says, and so grows and becomes the kind of person both he himself and God want him to be. In a relationship where you truly love another person and that love is expressed in many ways, holding him accountable is a powerful demonstration of love's depth.

Apart from love, without the kind of personal relationship that permits sharing and the expression of concern, attempts to hold another person accountable are viewed as manipulation, as coercion; and they are resented.

So we're driven back, in our discussion of motivation, to the truly basic issue. Do you, teacher, love your students? Do you know them as persons, share their lives, and share your life with them? Have you expressed your love by finding ways to be with them? To have them with you when you do, living out your faith? To show them that you are with them when *they* do? Do you go beyond the class to lead learners to a disciplined doing of God's Word, ensuring that they will experience reality, and in experiencing life as God meant it to be, grow to know and love Christ fully? If so, the final step is to hold them accountable for living by God's Word and to open your life in return that they might hold you accountable to them.

## The class as motivator

Before we leave this vital aspect of your teaching ministry, it's important to note that motivating response beyond the classroom is a ministry you can share with your students.

That is, in a very real way, your students, particularly if you teach teens or adults, can become involved in helping each other move beyond understanding of what God's Word says, to a personal, obedient response.

In the last chapter, I noted that when your students are sharing and discussing in class ways the Bible truth you're exploring applies to their lives, the implications of God's Word for each member of the class are more likely to be seen. So having an interactive class helps all members of the class to *hear* what God is saying.

In this chapter, I've outlined some ways in which your students can be motivated to *do* what the Word of God is saying. Being with you and being with you while *you* do, are primary motivators. The power of example, the authority of the authentic life, is central in motivating learner response to Jesus Christ. These dimensions of motivation are those that you, the teacher, must take full responsibility to provide. But as the students begin to respond and experience scripture reality, as they become more and more ready to do God's words, then they can begin to provide for each other some of the "be with them as *they* do" support that is so vital and encouraging. And they can also learn to be accountable to each other, to stimulate continuing response to God by checking up on each other in love and concern.

It takes time for you to develop the kind of relationship with your students that communicates love to them. It takes more time to develop a climate of openness and sharing in the classroom, in which lives are exposed to and examined in the light of God's Word. It takes time to be with your students, and time to express your faith in action while bringing them along with you.

What this means to you and me as teachers is that we should not expect our classes to turn around suddenly and become just like Naomi overnight. It means that we need to be willing to wait to see God working, even though it may take months. And it means that we need to take the right steps, working along with God the Holy Spirit, to communicate the love of Christ which alone transforms hearts. As God does express His love through our lives to our students, makes real His Word in us and in them, and frees them to do the Word by His powerful Spirit, all of us together—students and teacher and learners alike—will be knit together in a loving community of believers who are committed to loving and obeying Jesus Christ and to helping each other live out our shared commitment to Him.

## REACT

1. The elements in motivating response, which I have presented, are listed below. Check your understanding by briefly jotting down what each element involves on your part and your students' part.
   a. Be with them.
   b. Do, and have them with you.
   c. As they do, be with them.
   d. As they do and you do, hold each other accountable.

## ACT

1. Evaluate your own relationship with your class. At what stage of development are you now? That is, do you know them as persons, and are they getting to know you? Are you together as you express your faith in a practical way, involving them with you? Or are they doing, and so need to know that you are truly with them? Just how would you characterize the present state of your class?
2. Your evaluation of the class (above) not only points out its needs, but should also give you direction in moving to meet the needs. The reason for this is that these are **progressive stages** in the development of the class relationships. **Each stage presupposes the successful development of the previous one!** Thus, when you determine where your class members are, you also know what you need to do to help them grow beyond it.

   Based on your evaluation of the class you presently teach and your relationship with them, and based on the suggestions in this chapter, what do you need to do now?

# 9
In Our Sunday School?

Really, I started teaching them doctrine. I told the pastor that I felt my girls needed to know as much about God as they could, because how could they trust Him if they didn't know what he was like? So I started with sovereignty, and we spent weeks and weeks on just one story—the story of Daniel when he was telling Nebuchadnezzar about the dream, and how God showed Nebuchadnezzar that He **really** was sovereign; but He was so patient with him—a whole year after that dream before—well, you know.

I was very concerned about the fact that after opening exercises, by the time we got to class, got roll taken, Bibles counted, and so on, I'd have half an hour. The other teachers were saying, "Can't we take the kids out to play? What are we going to do for half an hour? The story is only ten minutes." And I was just terribly frustrated because I didn't have **enough** time.

We don't have to read much of Naomi's story before we realize that she's a very unusual teacher—and, perhaps, therefore we have doubts and questions. Can a teacher like Naomi fit in *our* Sunday school? Can I be a teacher, a *real* teacher, with things the way they are now?

We have to face questions like these and realize that often doubts and hesitation are rooted in the facts about the situation in which we minister, facts that include limitations of time and space, the curriculum we use, and even the others who minister with us in our departments. In looking at our situations realistically, we do wonder whether we can do things just the way Naomi did.

*Time.* This was one thing Naomi really struggled with. What she wanted to do—to get to know her girls, to involve them in a sharing kind of teaching and learning, to make sure they understood the biblical facts and worked together to relate them to their lives—all this took more time than the short Sunday school "hour" permitted. Naomi's response was to seek permission to have her girls for the whole hour (skipping departmental openings and activities) and finally to ask for, and get, an hour and a half by extending the Sunday school period into church time.

But this isn't always possible. While more and more churches are moving to "extended hour" teaching (keeping children with the same teacher all morning, through the traditional Sunday school period and the adult worship service), and while other churches are extending the Sunday school ten minutes to provide seventy rather than sixty minutes total time, far more churches cling tightly to the traditional time and to whole-school or multidepartment worship services that eat into class time and use up thirty or even forty precious minutes.

And, if you're a teacher, if you love your class members and want real involvement with them, you know that you simply can't get to know them well and develop a sharing climate in the time you have.

*Curriculum.* Naomi had serious problems with her curriculum too. She felt frustrated, because the materials seemed to rush so quickly through stories that, as she studied them carefully at home, seemed rich with meaning for her and for her girls. Naomi's response was to ask permission from her department superintendent and the pastor to develop her own curriculum—to teach what she felt her girls needed most.

This too is a course not everyone will want to take. It is certain, though, that every teacher will want to evaluate his or her curriculum materials carefully and to understand what curriculum can and cannot do.

So, what *is* the value of a curriculum? There are several values to a good one. First, Bible passages are selected by curriculum writers on the basis of the known needs of each age-group. And the passages are selected to cover a *range* of needs over the span of the curriculum cycle. It's true that at times special needs will surface in any class. One of the students has a need or raises a problem, and the group honestly wants help in finding God's guidance and direction. When this happens a teacher should, of course, forget the program and deal with the surfacing needs. After all, we are called to teach *people,* not to follow inflexibly a particular sequence of lessons. But while people always take precedence, a good curriculum can help us keep aware of the range of needs our students may have and help us avoid getting into the rut of teaching only our favorite themes and passages.

There are other criteria by which we want to evaluate curriculum, of course. It's not only important that the selection of Bible passages and the focus on age-group needs be solid; it is important that the curriculum structure the teaching-learning situation effectively. By this I mean that the four processes described in chapter seven be developed through the lesson structure.

Increasingly today curriculum materials are based on a solid philosophy of teaching-learning, and increasingly suggested teaching methods, visuals, discussion questions, and so on, are designed to help you, the teacher, involve your students in these four processes. If you are a new teacher, or if the sharing-teaching concept I've suggested in this book is new to you, good curriculum materials can provide really helpful suggestions for gaining and directing pupil involvement. In choosing a curriculum, awareness of its philosophy of teaching-learning is utterly basic.

Curriculum materials, then, need not be rejected in order for you to become the kind of teacher described in this book. You can and probably should use them to help you develop your teaching skill. But if you are truly to be a teacher, your curriculum materials will remain an aid and not become a crutch. They'll never replace a careful and prayerful study of the Bible itself in preparation for your class. And rather than slavishly following a lesson plan or sequence, you'll seek the guidance of the Holy Spirit as to what and how to teach each week, and guard your freedom to respond in obedience to the Spirit as He leads.

*Other teachers.* One of the greatest concerns Naomi had as she stepped out to teach differently was the failure of the other teachers in her department to understand or share her vision. While the others complained of too much time to tell the story, Naomi was frustrated with too little time to share in Christ.

It's hard to walk with others in a ministry unless you are agreed. Many of the changes Naomi wanted to make in her class situation were impossible, as long as the others felt so differently about the nature of their teaching task. If you are a teacher who wants to know and share with your class, to dig deeply into the Word and explore with your students its meaning for all your lives, and the others who minister with you see a need only to "tell the story, and that only takes ten minutes!"—well, you do have a problem.

Naomi solved this problem one way. She asked permission to go it alone when the others couldn't seem to understand her burden. And God did open doors for her. She taught—creatively and in depth—in a Sunday school like yours and mine, but alone.

Another way to solve this problem is to find others in the department where you teach to share your burden. To find others who feel Christ's love compelling them to go beyond the job to minister to persons. I feel that many in our Sunday schools today really want to teach and reach their children, youths, or adults; but so many do not understand who they are as teachers, or how to communicate the reality of God's Word to others and motivate them to experience it.

It's because I do believe that there *are* many who truly want to teach that I've written this book, to help them think through just who a teacher of the Word of God is to be, if he is to teach with conviction and power and in reality. So there *are* others; others in your school, others who want to do more than "take a class," others who want to minister God's Word and God's love to people.

Finding these others is an important step in strengthening your whole Sunday school and in building your own ministry. You can go it alone and try to buck the currents that are against you. But in your ministry you need, just as your students do, others to support and encourage you. You need others who share the same vision, who will pray and work with you in a team.

Naomi came to the point in her relationship with God where she felt ineffective as a teacher, but "I wanted Him, through the Holy Spirit, to teach those kids and let me be involved in the learning." If you are at this point yourself, share your desire with others. Ask God to use your sharing to give you one or two who are like-minded. As you pray with them and share what God is doing in each of your teaching ministries, as you encourage each other to deeper faith and obedience, trust God to infect others on your staff through you with your vision and your love. Trust God to build a team of teachers, who together will dedicate themselves to pouring their very lives into the lives of those they teach, and thus lead them to know reality in Jesus Christ.

## Not a job, a ministry with people

In everything I've said in this chapter, it's important to remember that we're looking at teaching not as a job, or a Sunday morning role, but as a ministry with people.

Even if your Sunday school conditions are very, very far from ideal, the basic elements for a teaching ministry are present: you, the teacher; they, the learners; the Bible, God's Holy Word; and the Holy Spirit, God Himself, who is able to work through each element with transforming power to communicate Jesus' life to all.

So the place to start in your teaching ministry isn't with the problems. It's not with trying to change the amount of time you have, or the way the opening is run, or the curriculum, or the people who work with you. The place to start in your teaching ministry is with you yourself in your own relationship with Jesus Christ and your own relationship with His Book. Seek God's love, that His Spirit might fill you with concern for the boys and girls, the young men and women, or the parents or grandparents that you teach.

The place to start in any ministry is with your own commitment to Christ, and then your commitment to other people for Jesus' sake, to the people He has called you to teach.

And *this* is possible, for you, in your Sunday school.

This is possible—now.

## REACT

1. What conditions in your Sunday school might help or hinder you in developing the kind of teaching ministry that I have described in this book? Briefly record them, jotting down your thoughts.
2. Think of all the fellow-teachers who minister with you in your department or in other departments of your Sunday school. Who do you believe might share your vision and concern for teaching? Who might join you as members of a team, to pray and encourage each other in your ministries?

## ACT

1. I trust God has been speaking to you as you read this book, even as He has been speaking to me as I write it. Why not take time for specific prayer, asking God to show you how He wants you to grow as a teacher, and where you can become more responsive to Him.
2. Pray too about your whole school, that God might use you to encourage other teachers to develop a more personal ministry with their students and build a team of men and women dedicated to guiding students into an experience of the reality that Scripture both reveals and invites us to experience in Christ.

# 10
## You, the Teacher

I wasn't really in a teaching position. . . .
I told the Lord . . . that I wanted Him, through
the Holy Spirit, to teach those kids and let me
be involved in the learning.

It's frightening to realize what being a teacher of God's Word involves.

It's frightening, because I realize it is so far beyond me. I can't share. Lord, I'm ashamed to reveal my inadequacies. I cannot love. Lord, so seldom do I really care about the persons in my class. Lord, I'm so indifferent; I don't know anything of Calvary love.

And to be with them? I don't have time, Lord, and I really don't want to make time. I have so many things I want to do and have to do, and it seems such a bother.

And this bit about being an example. I'm such a poor example. Lord, how can I live with others and have them look at *me* to see what You're like? Lord, I'm not even disciplined about my own times in the Word, or in my prayer life.

Lord, it's so frightening to think of being a teacher.

Yes, it is frightening, until I remember Jesus, until I remember that apart from Him I can do *nothing,* but in Him, "I can do all things through Christ which strengtheneth me." It's frightening, until I remember, "He is able to do exceeding abundantly above all that we ask or think, *according to the power that worketh in us"* (Eph 3:20, KJV). And then I realize that God is able to take even me and, by His Spirit, make me a teacher.

God is able to take my life and love others through me; to take my actions and show the reality of His Word through me; to take my involvement with my students and motivate them to respond to Him.

And He is able to do exactly this—for exactly the same reasons—with you.

Somehow, when I remember Jesus, I'm not afraid of all the hard things written here, or of the challenges of teaching that ask far more than I can ever bring. For the God who called us to teach, He is God. He can take me, and He can take you, and *He* can teach our classes, while He graciously lets us be "involved in the learning."

When I look at myself, I draw back from teaching. But when I look to Jesus, when I know His power and His love, the call to teach God's Word opens up to me as the most exciting invitation I could ever receive. For that's exactly what it is to be a teacher.

To accept God's invitation to teach His Word rightly is to step out beyond ourselves and begin a unique adventure with Him.